# FOR SUCH A TIME AS THIS

# FOR SUCH A TIME AS THIS

Sharing in the Mission of God Today

## ROY WILLIAMSON

*Foreword by the Archbishop of York*

DARTON · LONGMAN + TODD

First published 1996 by
Darton, Longman and Todd Ltd
1 Spencer Court
140–142 Wandsworth High Street
London SW18 4JJ

ISBN  0–232–52114–X

A catalogue record for this book is available
from the British Library.

Phototypeset by Intype, London
Printed and bound in Great Britain by
Page Bros, Norwich

To
C. Gordon F. Clark
my one time Vicar
and all time friend

'And who knows but that you
have come to royal position
for such a time as this.'

(Esther 4:14)

# Contents

# Acknowledgements

With thanks to my episcopal colleagues Peter, Martin and Wilfred and to all my other colleagues, ordained and lay, in the Diocese of Southwark who have inspired and encouraged me in the mission of God. In particular I am grateful to David Atkinson, Simon Barrow and Ann Stricklen for their advice and assistance, and Helen Mitchell and Andrew Nunn for their help in proof-reading.

Unless otherwise stated, all Bible quotations are taken from the New International Version of the Bible, published by Hodder & Stoughton Ltd, and are reproduced by permission.

The ASB version of the Sanctus, copyright © 1970, 1971, 1975 International Consultation on English Texts, is reproduced by permission of the Central Board of Finance of the Church of England.

### Study sessions

The study session material at the end of each chapter is designed to be used in small groups. The simple format can be adjusted to meet local needs and the contents can be used selectively. Though the material is primarily intended for group work, individuals may also find it helpful for personal reflection.

# Foreword

The Bishop as leader in mission was one of the clear priorities to which the Lambeth Conference 1988 drew attention as it sought to rehearse the constituents for any episcopal ministry towards the end of the 20th century and into the 21st.

Reading this new book of Bishop Roy Williamson leaves me in no doubt at all where his own personal priority is and where it always has been – the mission of God as reflected in and through the Church. Here is a Bishop in a hurry, with an urgency about the things of God, not only for the Church but for the sake of our society and nation. He draws refreshingly on the Scriptures – they have shaped who he is and how he thinks. It is a book based in the Bible and a book which brings the Bible alive through the way in which, along with and alongside the biblical quotations, references and allusions, he intersperses rich and varied and grounded experience in ministry.

And there is much sanctified common sense here which the Church needs to hear; he draws on a ministry which has spanned parochial, archidiaconal and episcopal as well as the cultural diversity reflected in Northern Ireland, Bradford and Southwark.

Here is a book which with an outline for a study session at the conclusion of each chapter is ideal for any parish. It will certainly excite and enliven discussion, though more importantly it will challenge and move to action.

+ DAVID EBOR:

# Introduction

Mission is a fashionable word in today's Church. We hear
a lot about the need to propagate our faith in a complex
and changing world. In many and various ways since the
formation of the earliest Church, Christians have wrestled
with the call of Jesus to seek the Kingdom and respond to
its demands. Sometimes, today, in the way that mission is
spoken of, the impression is given that only now, after
two thousand years, has the Church discovered what it is
supposed to be about. It can be promoted in such a way as
to suggest that the Church, both national and local, was
not already engaged in mission, but only became so when
we arrived.

That is a mistake which I have tried to avoid in this short
volume. As a bishop in the Church of God I can only do
the work that God has called me to do because of the
faithfulness, vision and energy of those who have gone
before me. We all build on the foundations which others
have laid and we are part of a Church with many members
and many gifts. The Church is as diverse as the world in
which it is set. That is a cause not for concern but for
celebration. Such diversity must not be despised or
destroyed but allowed to flower towards a common purpose. I believe that purpose is mission.

Every time I go out of the front door of my home in Tooting Bec Gardens I am faced with three choices. I can turn left into the garage, but there's no exit. I can turn right into the garden, which is definitely the scenic route, but, surrounded as it is by a high brick wall, there is no encounter, certainly not with people. My third choice is to go straight ahead and out through the front gate. That takes me immediately into one of the most air-polluted areas in the country, into a well-known and obvious red-light district of South London, and into all the challenges and opportunities presented by today's urbanised society.

It also takes me into that part of the world-wide Church of God known as the Diocese of Southwark. It is rich in diversity, a true microcosm of society. Indeed, the total spectrum of the nation's social, secular, cultural and religious life can be found there. That's the reason I prefer the front gate to either the garage or the garden!

It leads to encounter and engagement with the world which, with all its complexity and potential for good and evil, God loves. It was into this world that he sent his Son to serve and save. This is the world in which God has chosen to place his Church. His purpose is not that the Church should *withdraw* from the world, nor that it should *conform* to the world but that it should, with the help of his Holy Spirit, *share* in his mission to the world. This is the basic theme of this book.

Both at home and abroad I have discovered the joy and thrill of all sections of the Church – bishops, priests, deacons and laity – and all ecumenical partners within the Church, working together in the mission of God. A recent stimulating experience in the beautiful city of Melbourne has reinforced the value of such a creative partnership for mission no matter where we are in God's world.

As a bishop I have perceived my task as pursuing that mission in a manner that is true to me and pertinent to the times – and in such a way that affirms rather than decries what is already happening in the lives of individuals and worshipping communities throughout the Church and the country.

Every situation will be different. Each will call for specific priorities in mission. Thinking of my own ministry in Nottingham, Bradford and London, I know this to be the case. Those situations outlined in the pages which follow are sufficiently broad for most churches throughout the country to identify with and to use as a framework for study and action. It is for this reason that I have included some points for meditation, thoughts for reflection and questions for discussion and action at the end of each chapter.[1]

I hope that *For Such a Time as This* may become a source of inspiration, encouragement and challenge to churches eager to give a sharper focus to their mission priorities. Those priorities presented here bring mission within the reach of all. Mission is the calling of the whole people of God. *I long, therefore, that we might not just talk about it but get on and do it with conviction and compassion.*

Such practical involvement will need to be inspired by the vision of an amazingly generous and gracious God who reaches out in love towards all people with his gift of *shalom* – that wholeness, harmony, peace and well-being that only he can give. It will need to be empowered by his creative Spirit, who alone can renew our lives, worship and witness. He is himself the director of the whole mission enterprise. And it will need to take as its model the example of the one whose life personified mission and whose words, 'As the Father has sent me, I am sending you', forever links our mission with his.

I firmly believe that prayer is at the heart of all our work for God. *Prayer forms the basis of the mission priorities outlined in this book.* It is not without significance, therefore, that they have been summed up in the following prayer:

Spirit of Love, Spirit of Truth, Spirit of Christ, renew
   your whole church in its worship, work and witness.
Give us grace to seek first your kingdom and your
   righteousness.
Help us to share the faith, search for truth, serve our
   neighbour and confront injustice.
Inspire each of us for our part in the mission of God,
   and enable us to follow Jesus in his suffering love for
   the salvation of all people.[2]

The mission is God's. He calls all his people to share in
it. May he also give us all grace to live up to our calling.

*He insists on leading his people (us)
across all sorts of barriers, all kinds of
frontiers, TOWARDS THE WORLD.*

*P15-16*

*At CREATION — He sent his Spirit +
his Word — TO THE WORLD.*

*In BETHLEHEM — He sent the
incarnate Word — TO THE WORLD.*

*At PENTECOST — He sent the
Spirit — TO THE WORLD*

*Jesus is God's 'YES' to the world
— 'YES' — I love you 'YES' — I forgive you
'YES' — I save you. 'YES' I empower you
God is a God-for-people.*

# 1

# Under Starter's Orders

## The priority of mission

God and mission are inseparable. It is of the very nature of a God who is love to reach out in care and compassion towards the world he has created. 'Mission is God's "yes" to the world. It is the good news that God is a God-for-people, his self-revelation as the One who loves the world.'[1] Mission is a priority for the Church because God is a missionary God. That is the burden of this chapter. That is the theme of this book.

*[handwritten annotation: ∴ inevitable]*
*[handwritten annotation: as in Jesus]*

The scriptures – both Old and New Testaments – portray God as a missionary God and his people as called to be a missionary people. Indeed, 'The mission question is intrinsic to the Bible.'[2]

### Old Testament seeds

At first glance the Old Testament seems an unlikely place to find the seed-beds of mission. Israel was a people whose history tended to separate them from their neighbours. Their attitude at times was at best dismissive and at worst ruthless. Their sacred books laid stress on their exclusive calling to be God's chosen people. Even to this day the

Jewish faith contains no missionary programme towards non-Jews, unlike Islam and Christianity. Yet a careful reader can detect signs that the eyes of Israel were being lifted above the horizons of exclusivity towards a universal mission that would include the Gentile world. God's call to Abraham was a case in point.

> 'I will make you into a great nation
>     and I will bless you;
> I will make your name great,
>     and you will be a blessing . . .
> and all peoples on earth
>     will be blessed through you.'
>
> (Genesis 12:2)

Privilege and responsibility went hand in hand. Abraham was specifically called by God in order that the nations would be blessed. A nation, Israel, was called in order that a world would reap the benefits of the knowledge of God. The purpose of God's election of Israel was so that they would serve. Whenever service is withheld election loses its meaning. God's compassion is not restricted to Israel, it embraces the nations.

This insight into the purpose of Abraham's call and Israel's election, namely, the blessing of the nations, got lost for some time but it came back strongly in Second Isaiah's vision of Israel as a light to the nations: 'I will make you to be a covenant for the people and a light for the Gentiles' (Isaiah 42:6).

The manner in which the servant in Isaiah is to be a light to the nations is revealing. He brings God's light to the nations by attracting them to him. 'Israel is to let God's light flood through her own life. She is to show in her life what God can do with a people, and thereby invite them to seek him.' A careful study of the call of Abraham suggests a similar purpose. This is how the original promise to Abraham was to work. 'God would bless Abraham in a spectacular way to show what he could do for a man. If Israel lets God's light fill her life, this will make her a beacon which attracts the nations to her. God's people are expected thus to attract others to him.'[3]

Ultimately, of course, it is not Israel who has to do this. It is God who does it. She only has to be available to him. It is because she is open to the Spirit of the Lord coming upon her that she can be the bringer of light to the nations.[4] God doesn't send Israel on a proselytizing mission. In the power of his Spirit he wishes her life to be attractive. According to Isaiah, God is himself 'the missionary' who attracts the nations to him:

And foreigners who bind themselves to the Lord to
    serve him . . .
these will I bring to my holy mountain
and give them joy in my house of prayer . . .
for my house will be called a house of prayer for all
    nations.

(Isaiah 56:6–8)

Mission, in its broadest sense, was not missing from the Old Testament. There may be an emphasis on the preservation of the identity, solidarity and purity of Israel, but there are also clear indications that God was not bound by national and cultural frontiers but was able and willing to cross them in the cause of a universal mission. He is not only Israel's God. He is God of all the world.

*Barriers - for crossing!*
*get on common ground.*

*The church exists by mission as a fire exists by burning P10.*

## New Testament growth

If the music of that universal mission is in a somewhat minor key in the Old Testament it breaks forth into a major key, and in an increasing crescendo, in the pages of the New Testament and, particularly, in the person and work of our Lord Jesus Christ. It is true that the Early Church continued to remain within the fold of Judiasm for some considerable time. It is also true that the ministry of Jesus was carried out almost exclusively within the framework of Jewish religious faith and life. Nevertheless, early Christianity developed a world-wide missionary perspective of which Jesus was the primary source. He reflected the missionary mind of God in that he was 'the sent One', even though that initial sending was to the Israelite community. To that community he came preaching the Kingdom of God and challenging 'the attitudes, practices and structures that tended arbitrarily to restrict or exclude potential members of the Jewish community'.[5]

But it is clear that his concern was not only for those who were being marginalised by the Jewish establishment – the poor, the blind, the lepers, the hungry – but also for those who were beyond the boundaries of Israel.[6] Indeed much of his challenge and rebuke to the Israelite community was directed at their failure to fulfil the wider call of God regarding their responsibility towards the Gentile world. The incredible inclusiveness of the mission of Jesus spoke volumes. He was for ever crossing the boundaries between individuals and between groups. Why he ate with tax-collectors and sinners, for example, was a matter that puzzled the religious leaders of his day. It wasn't so much that Jesus had a personal programme of mission to the Gentiles. Rather, it was his whole life that made a statement which laid the foundations for Gentile mission. His use of the banquet theme in his teaching is a case in point.[7]

Gentiles are the 'substitute guests'; they take the place of those who refused the invitation to come. Again, it is the faith of a Gentile centurion that draws forth his amazed statement, 'I tell you the truth, I have not found anyone in Israel with such great faith' (Matthew 8:10). And, perhaps, it is Gentiles who are prefigured in the well-known story of the prodigal son, a story that Jesus tells in response to the carping criticism of the company he was keeping and the welcome he was expressing in eating with tax-collectors and sinners.[8]

Thus in story and statement, in attitude and in action, Jesus was raising the level of vision across the boundaries of Israel towards the Gentile world. What Israel, despite its privileged position was failing to do, Jesus, in his person and work, succeeded in doing and called his Church into being to do. The life, death and Resurrection of Jesus, together with God's gift of the Holy Spirit at Pentecost, resulted in the formation of a Church, the new community of faith, motivated towards mission beyond the boundaries of Israel. And while we must not detach our Lord's great commission – 'Go and make disciples of all nations . . . And surely I am with you always, to the very end of the age' – too much from the total context of that Gospel in which it is recorded, it nevertheless gives clear signals, confirmed by other parts of the New Testament, that the mission of God was to be pursued to the end of the world and the end of time.[9]

The mission of Jesus and the mission of the Church are indivisible. He has been called the catalyst that triggered its missionary consciousness. He was the one who provided and shaped its missionary statement. The post-Resurrection message to the Church was, 'he goes before you'. The challenge that faced and inspired the post-Pentecost Church was that the Spirit of God was alive and active in his world and that the Church should set aside any reluctance or hesitancy regarding mission and, with a sense of urgency, hurry after and try to catch up with God's Spirit.

Nowhere is this sense of urgency in universal mission more powerful than in the writings of St Paul. Before his amazing conversion on the Damascus road he is portrayed as one whose religious vision was narrowly limited to the cause of Israel. His encounter with the risen Jesus began to change all that. It created in him a world vision that sent him across geographical, cultural and ideological boundaries to proclaim the gospel, share the faith and plant churches. His desire was to preach the gospel where it had not been preached before. His commission came from the risen Christ. The mission he promoted was God's. It was universal in scope and urgent in tone. The motivation for it is probably best summed up in these words, 'Christ's love compels us', or as the NEB puts it so graphically 'The love of Christ leaves us no choice'.[10] There was a divine compulsion that sent Paul and his companions, despite hardship, persecution and the threat of martyrdom, outwards and onwards in mission. As far as they were concerned it was part of the *raison d'être* of the Church 'The Church exists by mission as a fire exists by burning.'[11]

## A surprising hesitancy

In the light of these things it is a little surprising that so many in today's Church still need to be convinced of the priority of mission. There is often a hesitancy, if not a reluctance, to engage in the task or to grapple with the challenge of it. Of course people rarely speak against mission: how could they in view of the overwhelming testimony of the scriptures? Nevertheless, all too frequently it is pushed down the Church's agenda by so-called more pressing needs. In the pursuit of God's mission the Church, far from having wings on its feet, so often gives the impression of having lead in its boots. Over the years, as I have sat in church committees, PCC meetings, local synods and even in General Synod, I have been conscious of the contrasting attitudes to mission. Within two minutes of a person standing up to speak on the subject you can tell whether or not he or she is for the identity and survival of the Church as an institution or for the cause of universal mission at any cost. Again, it rarely comes out as starkly as that. It is hedged around with all kinds of wise and modulated words about sensitivity and caution. But at the end of the day the message is often loud and clear – we must put our own house in order before we go offering help or meddling in the lives and affairs of other people.

But perhaps things are getting better. During the past ten years I have noticed a distinct change. Wherever I go churches are 'getting ready' for mission and evangelism. Indeed it would be easy to gain the impression in some quarters that the Church is in a state of perpetual preparation for mission. This is not said in a spirit of criticism. As one who over the years has ministered in seven different parishes, I recall vividly, and with not a little ruefulness, that my strategy was so often geared to preparing for mission rather than doing it. There always seemed to be something to be put right first before the way was clear to get on with the task. And so I convinced myself that . . . when I had reordered the Church, replaced the pews with chairs and the choir with a music group; when I had moved the font and made room for coffee to be served after the service; when I had trained my people to the uttermost and installed all the latest technological equipment . . . then . . . then we would be ready for outreach in mission and evangelism. Then things would begin to happen. Then the vision would

be realised. I always seemed to be leading a local church
that was getting ready for mission.

I was watching television recently when there was horse-
racing from one of our well-known racecourses. As I
watched the horses milling around the starting stalls before
the race began I suddenly had a flight of fancy: how like the
Church and its problems about getting ready for mission
and evangelism. An important race is on, but the horses
are reluctant to go into the stalls. In fact the attempt to get
them into place takes days rather than minutes and the
jockeys, owners, trainers, stewards, starters and even pun-
ters and bookies are all to be found trying to persuade,
nudge or equip the horses to enter the stalls. Even the
horses are busy nudging each other: 'We need all the tal-
ents, all the gifts, all the riches of all kinds of horseflesh in
this race. I'm ready to go myself but I've just stepped out
of line for a minute or two to help you get ready.' Many
are getting ready. Others are prevaricating. All need to come
'under starter's orders'.

In my experience the fantasy is just a little too near the
truth for comfort. There is always something else to do.
The time is never quite right. The prevailing circumstances
are not conducive. A sense of urgency is replaced with
wishful thinking. If only the Church Commissioners hadn't
lost all that money. If only the Church hadn't been preoccupied with the ordination of women. If only we were like the
Early Church, uncluttered with bureaucracy. If only we
were better organised. If only we prayed more. If only our
Church leaders were more prophetic. If only there was a
Wilberforce or a Wesley. If only the Churches were united.
In other words, if only the times were different, mission
wouldn't be a problem. But, of course, if we believe that
we will believe anything.

## No time like the present

The truth is that we are living in the only time we have got. God has chosen today's Church for today's task. It is a slightly terrifying thought but a source of enormous encouragement and exciting challenge. Many of you will recall the intensely moving and highly emotional pressure that came upon Esther in the book that bears her name. At the heart of that interesting story of intrigue when the Jewish nation was under threat of extermination, a young Jewish girl who had become queen, after what was probably the first ever beauty contest, is exhorted by Mordecai her cousin to prevent such a disaster by using her privileged position to win the king's favour and to save her people. 'Who knows', said Mordecai, 'but that you have come to royal position for such a time as this.'[12]

God has called us into his Church 'for such a time as this'. We may wish the circumstances were different but it is a waste of time to do so. I had this truth burned into my heart when I was an incumbent of a parish church in the Midlands. I had been asked to unite and lead two small congregations whose church buildings, having been declared redundant, had been demolished. For a period of three years we worshipped in an infant school, setting up our religious symbols and all the traditional accoutrements of worship each Sunday morning.

During this period one man was missing. He was a person of influence and ability who had been a fairly regular worshipper in one of the churches before the building was demolished. He adamantly refused to worship with us in the infant school. 'I don't consider that to be a church. When you build your new church I will return,' he said, 'but not until then.' Three years later he was invited to the opening of the new church. An hour before the dedication service was due to begin the sad news came through that he had died earlier that morning. His was the first funeral service to be conducted in the new church! He had kept his promise to return but he had run out of time.

## God's special time

I recall that true story not to introduce a note of either sensationalism or emotionalism. On the contrary I want simply to emphasise a sober truth that the time we have available to us now is the only time that is guaranteed to us. It is the special time God has given to us. We are accountable for our use of it. God has not been taken unawares by the particular circumstances, demands or challenges currently confronting the Church, nor is he ignorant of our inadequacies. He knows that we carry his treasure 'in pots of earthenware' but we have been called for such a time as this. One of the great biblical words for 'time' is the Greek work *kairos*. It carries a great variety of shades of meaning, including 'the right time', 'the point of opportunity', 'the favourable moment'. It is used in the New Testament with reference to a great welter of different situations. The concept of God's 'special' time is also found in the Old Testament. But with the coming of Jesus, as the New Testament makes clear, 'a unique *kairos* has dawned, one by which all other time is qualified'.[13]

Mark 1:15, which Professor Jeremias declares to be the keynote of Jesus' proclamation, makes this clear: 'The hour of fulfilment has dawned, the reign of God is already being manifested here and now; soon the catastrophe introducing its definitive coming will arrive. Make use of the time before it is too late: it is a matter of life and death.'[14] While these words have special reference to the Kingdom of God, the *kairos* of which they speak has implications for the mission of the Church. Now is the time, the point of opportunity, the favourable moment for the mission of God through today's Church.

The fact that the Church is said to be in crisis is no excuse for a failure to engage in mission. Everywhere one goes today someone is proclaiming the Church to be in crisis, as though that was a unique and disastrous position for the Church to be in. But it was the missionary statesman Hendrik Kraemer who said, 'Strictly speaking, one ought to say that the Church is always in a state of crisis and that its greatest shortcoming is that it is only occasionally aware of it.' He argued that this ought to be the case because of 'the abiding tension between the Church's essential nature and its empirical condition'[15] – between what it is and what it is called to be. The Church has always needed apparent failure and suffering in order to become more alive to its real nature and mission. Crisis, far from being a debilitating factor, should provide the Church with the opportunity of truly being the Church and becoming what it is called to be – a Church in mission.

## The context of mission

But what is the context and the content of this mission to which the Church is called? The context in which the Church is set is the world. The Church belongs within the context of the world because the Lord of the Church is also the Lord of the world. Mission has its origin neither in the Church at large nor in a special group within the Church. It has its origin in God who, as we have seen, is a missionary God who insists on leading his people across all kinds of frontiers towards the world. At Creation he sent his Word and his Spirit – to the world. In Bethlehem he sent the incarnate Word and at Pentecost the Holy Spirit – to the world. Mission is God giving up himself, laying aside his divine prerogatives and taking on humanity – for the sake of the world. Mission is God moving into the world in his Son and in his Spirit. The mission which originates in God, which took 'flesh' in his Son and is continued by his Spirit, is the same mission committed to his Church: 'As the Father has sent me, I am sending you' (John 20:21). The Church is essentially a missionary Church. There is no true Church unless it is engaged in mission. As Bonhoeffer said, 'The Church is only the Church when it exists for others'[16] Its mission is God's mission and it is directed towards God's world.

But the context and the content of that mission need to be brought into sharper focus if we are to participate in it with integrity and conviction. There is a tendency these days to describe practically everything the Church does as mission. Stephen Neill sounded a wise note of warning in his famous adage, 'If everything is mission, nothing is mission', and David Bosch, in his superb volume *Transforming Mission*, reminds us that 'mission' is virtually impossible to define. He sees it as a multi-faceted ministry involving witness, service, justice, healing, reconciliation, liberation, peace, evangelism, fellowship, church planting ... and much more.[17] But he has an anxiety, which we all need to share, lest we delineate mission too sharply and in doing so imprison and ensnare it within the narrow confines of our own predilections. The use of the word 'transforming' in the title of his book carries with it a dual application. Mission is an activity that transforms reality but there is a constant need for mission itself to be transformed. Indeed his book was written on the assumption that the definition of mission is a continual process of sifting, testing, reformulating and discarding.

If this assumption is correct, and I believe it is, it places great demands upon the Church and, if taken seriously, means that mission must be entered into not with complacency – 'let's do a bit of mission' – but with intellectual honesty and a willingness to listen and pay proper attention to what is happening in the world. Only then can we engage in mission with an integrity that will not be easily deflected and with a courage that is prepared to pay the price and be unafraid to admit failure.

## Diversity – a bridge or a barrier?

As a leader within the Church of God I find that one particular fact of ecclesiastical life can all too readily apply a very effective brake to the task of corporate mission. Diversity is part of the gift of God's Spirit to the Church. The kaleidoscopic nature of the Church is a rich resource. Through it the many-splendoured grace of God is revealed. But, if we are not careful, it can also be allowed to hinder mission. For the diversity of people in which we rightly rejoice also includes a diversity of theological emphasis which, sadly, some refuse to accept when it comes to mission. And so, for instance, we get the unedifying spectacle of some evangelical members of a congregation refusing to co-operate in mission with their Roman Catholic neighbours, and some Anglican churches with a charismatic emphasis reluctant to share in mission with those of a more liberal persuasion. And, a fairly recent development following the ordination of women to the priesthood, clergy declaring themselves to be 'out of communion' with their bishop and therefore, presumably, unable to join with him in a common mission. Even if all hold the so-called traditional biblical faith, some will want to lay emphasis on one particular aspect of that faith rather than another. This should not surprise any of us. Most of us on our Christian pilgrimage have found that specific aspects of the faith have risen to the surface of our consciousness at certain stages of the journey and shaped our life and motivated our service.

What is true of individuals is also true of churches, and, indeed, of the universal Church. Some will want to stress the Incarnation, others the Cross. Some will want to lay their emphasis on the Resurrection while others will prefer to concentrate on Pentecost or the Parousia. All such emphases are valid and important but none must be allowed to become detached from the others, otherwise the gospel we seek to communicate to the world will be truncated and the mission we offer distorted. Our mission is undergirded by and is a practical proclamation of the incarnate, crucified, resurrected, ascended Christ, who is present among us in his Spirit and who takes us with him into his future. As Bosch has so powerfully written, 'The shadow of the man of Nazareth, crucified under Pontius Pilate, falls on the glory of his resurrection and ascension, the coming of his Spirit and his parousia. It is the Jesus who walked with his disciples who lives as Spirit in his church; it is the crucified One who rose from the dead; it is the One who has been lifted up on the cross who has been lifted up into heaven; it is the Lamb slaughtered yet living who will consummate history.'[18]

## Getting our priorities right

Mission is far too important to be side-tracked by prolonged debates about different emphases within the biblical faith. The needs of the world are much too pressing to be pushed to the margins of the Church's life while it gets on with internal, esoteric and self-indulgent discussion. Of course, everything is not mission and other things besides mission are important. As we shall see in later chapters, the worship of God and the pastoral care of the faithful, the renewal of the people of God and their growth in holiness are all vital to the health and wholeness of the Church and to its effective mission. But we need to beware lest in due time the charge is levelled against us, 'You should have practised the latter without leaving the former undone.' (Luke 11:42)

There is a proper balance to be struck in today's Church just as there was in the apostolic Church. In its thrust towards the Gentile world it also had to bear in mind its own stability and religious identity. This was an issue that dominated the historical ministry of Jesus, indeed, 'the concern of his contemporaries for identity was punctured by Jesus' moves towards the outcasts and sinners'.[19] The Bible does more than take note of this inevitable balancing act between identity and mission. From the Christian perspective, at least, God's scale tilts in favour of outreach over identity. Jesus stands as the disturber of the status quo, as one who shatters the canons of propriety in the cause of an unexpectedly compassionate God.'[20]

If in Jesus we have the mission of God personified then some very challenging and somewhat disturbing factors need to be borne in mind if we are to accept his invitation to share in that mission with him. There are at least two major factors of which we need to take note.

The first is the cost factor. It is outlined in the words of our Lord to his disciples: 'If anyone would come after me, he must deny himself and take up his cross and follow me. For whoever wants to save his life, will lose it, but whoever loses his life for me and for the gospel will save it.' (Mark 8:34–35) And again: 'Unless a grain of wheat falls to the ground and dies, it remains only a single seed. But if it dies, it produces many seeds.'[21] What Jesus seems to

20

be saying here is that if he had been primarily concerned
for the preservation of his own life then God's transforming
mission towards the world would have been negated. It is
our Lord's dying that becomes life-giving and life-transforming. As it was with Jesus so it is with his Church. If,
faced with the increasing pressures that are undoubtedly
coming upon it today, it seeks to preserve its own life,
it will lose it and, in so doing, destroy the credibility
of its gospel and fail in its God-given responsibility towards
the world. We need to count the cost of being involved
deeply in the mission of God – and the cost of trying to
'opt out'.

Secondly there is the growth factor. It is not without
significance that the grain of wheat analogy was given by
Jesus at the very moment when the Greeks came looking
for him. At first glance it seems a surprising response to
the arrival of those who were asking to see him. One might
have expected Jesus at this moment to have launched into
a meaningful story or, perhaps, a Sermon on the Mount
kind of discourse. It seems strange for him, instead, to refer
to the Cross, for that is what his analogy of the wheat and
the reference to 'the hour' having come was all about. Jesus
knew that Greeks were lovers of wisdom, so he uses the
opportunity to stretch their minds and challenge their pre-
conceived ideas about public acclaim, power and achieve-
ment. What is the thing that will attract Greeks to Jesus?
What is it that will draw the whole world after Jesus? It will
not be done through his teaching or his acts of power, but
through his public humiliation as he is lifted up on the
Cross, followed by his being lifted up in Resurrection and
Ascension. Glory through humiliation, that was a category
of thought foreign to the Greeks for whom the Cross was
'foolishness'. Perhaps Jesus saw the coming of the Greeks
as a kind of 'first fruits' or anticipated harvest of the Gentile
world that would reap the benefits of his death and Resur-

rection in the cause of a universal mission. Was not this the double significance of his words in that same chapter, 'But I, when I am lifted up from the earth, will draw all men to myself'?

*universal mission*

I am not advocating that the Church should develop an unrealistic 'kamikaze' attitude towards mission. But I am trying to face the fact that, as in the case of Jesus, it will not be our power and success that will prove attractive and promote growth in mission and evangelism, but our vulnerability and sense of failure. The message of the grain of wheat and the Cross of Jesus is clear and consistent, life comes through death, power comes through weakness. It is in giving that we receive.

**IT IS IN GIVING THAT WE RECEIVE.**

## The open hand

Perhaps my point is best summed up in a simple illustration. When one of our sons was fifteen months old my wife and I took him to the seaside for a holiday. It was his first encounter with a beach full of fine silvery-white sand. He was fascinated by it and, picking up his first handful of sand, squeezed it tightly in his chubby little fist. But the tighter he squeezed the faster the sand ran out and he was left with an empty hand and a puzzled expression on his face. He tried again and the same thing happened. Whether by accident or design he got it right third time round. He scooped up the sand and, instead of squeezing it, held it out for us to see in the palm of his hand. We enjoyed his infant discovery of a parable of life and a pattern for mission. The blessings and the resources of God, including life itself, are not to be clasped selfishly to oneself. They are to be shared with others. An open hand rather than a closed fist is a true symbol of the incredibly generous, gracious

*SIMPLE!*

and compassionate God who offers us life and calls us to share in his life-transforming mission.

So away with hesitancy. Away with reluctance. Away with perpetual preparations. Let us catch the biblical vision of a missionary God who, through his Son and his Spirit, calls and equips his Church to carry on that mission onwards and into the third millennium. Let us rejoice in the diversity of the Body of Christ and use it creatively for the service of the world. And let us remember that our baptism, which initiated us into Christ, also initiated us into his mission. On the day of our baptism we, sacramentally, came under starter's orders for mission. So, '. . . let us throw off everything that hinders . . . and let us run with perseverance the race marked out for us . . . Let us fix our eyes on Jesus' (Hebrews 12:1–2).

## Study session

OPENING PRAYER

God of the open hand,
Enable us to receive your mercies with gratitude,
and to share them with generosity, sensitivity and
conviction.

READINGS

Isaiah 56:6–8; Hebrews 12:1–2.

MEDITATIONS

'Mission is ... the good news that God is a God-for-people.' (p. 5)

'The mission of Jesus and the mission of the Church are indivisible.' (p. 9)

'The Church exists by mission as a fire exists by burning.' (p. 10)

'God has chosen today's Church for today's task.' (p. 13)

'The Church belongs within the context of the world because the Lord of the Church is also Lord of the world.' (p. 15)

'The blessings and the mercies of God ... are not to be clasped selfishly ... they are to be shared with others.' (p. 21)


OUR EXPERIENCE

• Which activities and commitments of your church are most clearly an expression of God's mission, and why? (cf. list on p. 16)

• What are the biggest barriers to mission for your church? How can they be countered? (pp. 11–12)

• What is the difference between mission in the name of Christ and mission which actively honours Christ? (pp. 19–21)

CHRISTIAN RESPONSE

• Gather your answers to the three questions above on to three large sheets of paper, marked RESPONSES, BARRIERS and CHRIST'S WAY. Where do you see your current strengths, vulnerabilities and opportunities as a missionary church?

• What are the principle motives for mission? Consider the nature of God (pp. 5–7), the person of Christ (pp. 8–10 and 18–20), the needs of the world and the calling of the Church (pp. 14–18)

• 'The Church has always needed apparent failure and suffering in order to become more alive to its real nature and mission' (p. 15). How does this statement throw light on the missionary challenge facing the Christian Church in this country? Should we wait until we have put our own house in order? (p. 11)


ACTION

• Consider the motives, opportunities and context for the mission of your church and spell out three simple priorities for the coming year.

• Write up two or three examples of how your church is seeking to respond to the call to mission. Share them ecumenically and ask neighbouring churches to share their ideas and experiences with you.

CLOSING PRAYER

Redeeming God,
When the time was right you sent your son.
Send us, also, to be a living sacrifice
Shaped by Christ's will
And empowered by his love. Amen.

# Open to God

## A Church renewed for mission

Mission is a work of transformation. The Church, as an agent of mission, must itself be an example of God's transforming work. The renewal of the Church's own life, therefore, is not only vital for the work of mission, it is also necessary for its own integrity as an agent of that mission. In this chapter I draw attention to the need for renewal in three aspects of the Church's life. There are others, of course, and they will be dealt with elsewhere, but the renewal of worship, community, and partnership between clergy and laity is, I believe, of immense significance to the work of mission.

Mission begins with prayer. The cynic might see this as a further delaying tactic, a diversion from getting on with the real task, an excuse for not crossing the starting line. The reverse is true. Prayer is a reaching out towards God, an opening up of ourselves to him. It is an acknowledgement that mission, and the vision that motivates our involvement in it, springs from God. It is a recognition that the first call upon the Church and the individual Christian is not to evangelise, nor even to engage in mission, but to worship God. What happens in our churches on Sunday morning and, indeed, throughout the rest of the week, is of vital importance to the whole of our work of mission.

## Worship renewed

For years I have been inspired by the powerful statement from the Constitution on the Sacred Liturgy from the Documents of the Second Vatican Council. Though it is with special reference to the Catholic Mass, it encapsulates for me a vision for the worshipping life of the local and, indeed, the national church. 'The Liturgy is the summit toward which the activity of the Church is directed; it is also the fount from which all her power flows.' The statement creates in me both a vision and a longing that the event which we call worship will be sufficiently dynamic to transform the lives of the worshippers and to send them out to help transform the life of society around them. That's the vision. The reality, all too often, is very far removed from it. There are many glorious exceptions, of course, and I have discovered in tiny rural churches, as well as in inner-city and suburban churches, a transforming vibrancy that has little to do with the aesthetic nature of the building, the size of the congregation or the reputation of the minister. There has been an indefinable sense of the presence of God and his all-inclusive love, in the midst of which I have felt my own life touched and changed.

Sadly, however, this is often the exception rather than the rule. Of course I shall be in trouble for daring to say these things and members of my former parishes will be saying, 'Physician, heal thyself', but the matter is too urgent to be neglected. For over eighteen years, first as archdeacon and then as bishop, I have sat at what has been called 'the sharp end' of hundreds of churches, feeling like a spectator and waiting to 'do my bit' in the service. Again and again I have found myself thinking, 'What on earth am I doing here? If I didn't have to be here would I come voluntarily? What has all this got to do with life out there in the real world?' The answers to such questions have been too painful to contemplate but, frankly, there have been too many times when, at best, the worship has been uninspiring, at worst it has been downright boring. Yet the ministers have been excellent and the people have been warm, friendly and sincere. But the questions I have come away with have been these: 'What power has this liturgy and worship to change the lives of those who name the name of Christ in this community? What is life-transforming about this worship that would send this community of worshippers out with enthusiasm to be agents of that transformation within the wider society? What have they discovered about God that simply must be shared with the world around, because without it society cannot become whole?'

I wouldn't want to be misunderstood at this point. I am not equating so-called lively church services with life-transforming worship. I am not pleading for competent music groups or quality choirs, nor am I referring to worship which is charismatic or traditional, catholic or evangelical. It is something which may include all or none of these things but it is greater than them all. I hope it will not be dismissed as either too simplistic or too subjective when I say that it is much more a 'meeting of hearts' – God's and ours.

Worship, and its potential and power to transform, came alive for me when as a fairly young Christian I 'discovered' those amazing words of Jesus spoken to the woman of Samaria: '. . . true worshippers will worship the Father in spirit and truth, for they are the kind of worshippers the Father seeks' (John 4:23). It was those words, 'the Father seeks', that revolutionised my approach to liturgy and worship. I was staggered by the thought that God actually wanted me and sought me for this purpose! I am convinced, therefore, that when there is a fusion, as it were, between

our longing hearts and God's longing heart, our worship
becomes dynamic and alive with the life and Spirit of God.
It becomes creative. It opens up new visions of God, his
people and his world. It becomes life-changing, for our life
in the world is shaped and transformed by it.

## WORSHIP AND LIFE, A SEAMLESS ROBE

To put it another way, life-transforming worship becomes
possible where a community of faith is truly open to God's
Spirit and open to God's world: a community of people
whose life in the world is summed up in their worship
and whose worship in the Church is not divorced from their
life in the world; a community in which life and worship is
a 'seamless robe'; where people gather for worship fully
expecting the living God to meet with them and go from
worship in the conviction that by his Spirit the same living
God is going with them and before them; a conviction that
their life and work from Monday to Saturday is all of a
piece with their life and worship on Sunday.

  Whilst attending a priests' retreat many years ago I heard
the conductor, Michael Ramsey, a former Archbishop of
Canterbury, refer to the Eucharist as 'half an hour of earth
and half an hour of heaven'. He explained that we carry
into the Eucharist the things of earth, joys and sorrow,
hopes and fears, successes and failures; and suddenly we
find ourselves caught up in the worship of heaven, as 'with
angels and archangels and with all the company of heaven'
we sing,

> Holy, holy, holy Lord,
> God of power and might,
> heaven and earth are full of your glory.
> Hosanna in the highest.[1]

The late Archbishop was convinced and convincing in his belief that mission sprang from a vision of God communicated through worship. Perhaps that is why he saw the Eucharist not only as the gateway of heaven but also and, indeed, in consequence, the gateway into the suffering world all around us. On the Mountain of Transfiguration Peter and his companions were not permitted to linger, though they longed to do so, in the glory of the vision they had received. They were to go back down into valley where there was a mission to be accomplished in the shape of a diseased boy, a distressed and disappointed father and a community of faith that appeared impotent in the face of such need.[2] It was in the context of the valley that they were to catch glimpses of God's glory and give practical expression to the vision they had received on the mountain. That is the essence of mission. It begins with a vision of a God who is love and who invites us to participate in his work of transformation in every aspect of his world.

## Community renewed

Mission is a work of transformation and if the Church is called to be an agent of that transforming work then surely the Church must not only be open to, but increasingly reveal evidence of, this renewing power of God within its own life. 'Don't tell me, show me' is a legitimate demand. A Church which is open to God's Spirit is likely to reveal in its life a new concentration on Jesus Christ. A primary task of the Spirit, as Jesus indicated, is to 'Take from what is mine and make it known to you' (John 16:15). If a local community of Christians is truly open to the Spirit then the supreme characteristic of the life of Jesus, namely, the power of love, will increasingly shape and transform the life of that community. It is the Holy Spirit who pours the love of God into the hearts and lives of his people, thus giving them the basic equipment for mission, for, at its simplest, mission is love in action. 'The Mission of the Church is to put love where love is not.'[3] It is the good news of God's love, incarnated in the witness of a community, for the sake of the world. How vitally important it is, therefore, for the work of mission that the community of faith should be constantly renewed and transformed in love by being open to God's Spirit.

## HALLMARK OF OUR TIME

This is particularly so when we recognise that one of the great hallmarks of our time is a hunger for new community – a hunger which is created, perhaps, by the challenge of one of the great questions of our time, namely, 'How can people live together?' In the huge South London conurbation which forms part of the Diocese of Southwark there are upwards of two million people. Between them they speak some fifty languages and encompass a vast variety of cultural groups including people of faith and no faith. But where, in the midst of this amorphous multitude, are people to find a sense of belonging? Indeed, in such a context some would consider that the language of belonging is now obsolete.

It is a question not limited to South London. One of the by-products of urbanised life in the modern world is increasing anonymity. Surrounded by people of different cultures and faiths, living side by side with people we don't know, where and how do we belong? Certainly a nostalgic longing for the old-style community will only bring further frustration. It is dead and gone. Indeed, the death of community is the cause of so many of the painful challenges we face today in both Church and society, including the privatising and marginalising of faith. Hence the hunger for new community. We must respond to that hunger and find new ways of belonging or, at least, of travelling the road together.

In the light of these things one of the more exciting aspects of Church life today is that community is being rediscovered. Throughout this country, across the denominational divide and across the world, in a great variety of places and forms, community is developing. Communities like Taizé, Corrymeela, Columbanus and a host of others are, I believe, an expression of the hunger for community within the Church, to say nothing of society. But they are more than that. They are a recognition that Christians are not meant to journey alone. Faith flourishes most when it exists within community, a truth to which scripture, tradition and history bear ample testimony. I believe these are signs and pointers to the whole Church and, particularly, to each local expression of it, of the need for new community. Already there are some quite remarkable examples – I know of several within my own diocese – where local churches are developing a community life which is having a powerful and healing influence within the wider community. They are communities of faith which are (1) open to God's Spirit and (2) to God's world. They have recognised that community is not only important for its own sake but that the community is the primary bearer of mission. Mission does not proceed from a bishop or a synod, from a council or a committee, 'but from a community gathered around the word and the sacraments and sent into the world'.[4] And in a chronically alienated and divided society the Church, and the local community of faith, has a prophetic role in highlighting one of the ways in which people may learn not only to live together but also to travel together with hope.

But if the community of faith in the local church is to

be such a prophetic sign and symbol then it will have to acknowledge with humility that, like the Universal Church of which it is the local expression, it doesn't have all the answers. There is always a tension between the Christian community for which we long and the Christian community as it actually is. We must be realistic. The feeling of belonging and support which may exist within some of the new and exploratory communities is not easily achieved in a larger or gathered congregation. Nevertheless, the ideal and the actual community belong together. In the words of Bonhoeffer, 'He who loves the dream of a Christian community more than the community itself, often does great damage to that community, no matter how well-intentioned he may be'.[5]

Within the context of mission I believe this 'journey' or struggle of the Christian community, whether it be large or small, from what it actually is to what it is called to be is of significant importance. To give the impression that it has already arrived at its ultimate destination is not only foolish, it is false – and society knows it. If the community is open to God's world as well as to God's Spirit then it will need to be seen as it really is, a group of diverse and imperfect people struggling to travel together; a community held together by the conviction that the Jesus story is true and by the hope that they will one day 'grasp that for which they have been grasped'[6] and become what they really are – the Community of God.

BECOMING WHAT WE ARE

In the meantime, and with the help of God's Holy Spirit, the local as well as the national church must endeavour to become what it is called to be. In the next chapter we shall be looking more closely at matters concerning the Kingdom of God, but if the church community is in any way to be seen as a credible sign of the Kingdom it must bear some resemblance to it. It must become what it is called to be and what its foundation documents proclaim it to be.

The Church is a penitent community. Our anthem is first and foremost, 'Kyrie eleison, Christe eleison, Kyrie eleison' – 'Lord have mercy, Christ have mercy, Lord have mercy'. The Church is a body of people who recognise and accept that they have failed. 'We have left undone those things we ought to have done, and we have done those things we ought not to have done.'[7] This is also true in our personal lives; it is true in our families, in our local communities, our industries and politics. It is true nationally and internationally and we are sorry and publicly acknowledge our sins of omission and commission. We will all have our own theories as to why *Faith in the City*[8] proved to be such a powerful document. I believe it was because it had such a deep and sincere note of penitence. In it the Church recognised that there was a beam in its own eye, with regard to its work in Urban Priority Areas, before it sought to remove the mote in the eye of the nation. There is a key lesson for us here. God forbid that we should ever fail to be a penitent community.

The Church is a forgiven community. 'Though your sins be like scarlet they shall be as white as snow' (Isaiah 1:18). This truth is at the very heart of the Gospel – no wonder it is good news! Though we do not deserve it, God in Christ has enabled our sins to be forgiven. When humankind had flown in the face of God and crucified the Lord of glory, God's answer was not judgement but mercy: 'God raised Jesus from the dead . . . and exalted him to his own right hand as Prince and Saviour that he might give repentance and forgiveness of sins' (Acts 5:31). The Church is a body of people who know that the slate has been wiped clean and that they have been set free to live for God in the world. We must, therefore, live as people who know and have experienced that sense of liberation when the past has been sorted out under God. I believe that is the thought which lies behind the motivation for mission I mentioned in the first chapter, namely, 'the love of God leaves us no choice'. Another version has it, 'Christ's love compels us'. It is the same thing, the words mean a pressing together, a hemming in. My old college tutor used to illustrate this truth by his experience during his days in China of travelling by boat along a river. The river was sluggish as it went across the flat plains but when it came to a narrow gap the waters tumbled and roared with such force that the passengers had to hold on tightly. The power and compulsion came when the waters were hemmed in. It is when we are 'hemmed in' by the forgiving love of God in Christ that we are empowered by God's Spirit to break free from living for ourselves and set free to live for Christ and for others. 'My chains fell off, my heart was free, I rose, went forth and followed thee!'[9]

3) The Church is a forgiving community. We are required to forgive others, just as God has forgiven us. It was Archbishop Ramsey who, when asked by a bright young student in the midst of a university discussion what Christianity had to offer a modern technological society, replied, 'the forgiveness of sins'. It remains society's greatest need and the Church through its forgiven life can hold out to people this glorious possibility of a new beginning, of a fresh start. Our world cries out for people who have learned how to forgive one another and how to settle wrongs and not be consumed with enmity and bitterness. As a community of faith we need to guard against raising our own sophisticated thresholds that prevent those who need and want forgiveness, acceptance and healing from stretching out and touching the hem of Christ's garment. The Church community above all others ought to provide the environment

in which the forgiving love of God can bend back the
bruised reed to usefulness and strength, and can fan
the dimly burning wick until the stench stops and light and
warmth break forth once more.

The Church is an international community. It is a world-
wide family that transcends language, colour and culture.
But the Church in this country has still a long way to go
before this becomes a reality. The rich diversity of cultures
in the local community is not always reflected in the local
church. Yet one of the greatest signs of hope that we can
offer an increasingly individualistic society, and one which
is showing an unwelcome rise in racism, is an ability within
the Christian community to live in peace, righteousness
and justice with people of different cultures. I believe that
the Church in this country, at this particular stage of its
pilgrimage, needs to work harder at this aspect of community life than at any other. Perhaps the words of the old
rabbi are more pertinent than we imagined. In a teaching
session with some young disciples he asked them how they
knew that night had ended and the day was dawning.
'Could it be,' asked one, 'when you can see an animal in
the distance and tell whether it is a sheep or a dog?' 'No,'
replied the rabbi. 'Could it be,' asked a second, 'when you
can look at a tree in the distance and tell whether it is a fig
or an olive tree?' 'No,' the rabbi replied. 'Well, then, what
is it?' his young disciples pressed. 'It is when you can look
on the face of any woman or man and see that she or he is
your sister or brother. If you cannot do this, no matter what
time it is, it is still night!'

In South London and many other multi-cultural areas
there is an immensely practical and loving way of giving
expression to this truth that we belong to each other. White
Anglican churches, for instance, can learn from and celebrate insights from other (Anglican) ethnic groups: ways
of sharing the peace; musical traditions; styles of food

preparation for church gatherings; other cultural festivals. Love is paying attention to the other person.

The Church is a holy community. There are times when it neither looks like it nor feels like it. But the community of faith cannot avoid its calling to be 'holy as he is holy' (1 Peter 1:16). Despite its unworthiness the Christian community knows that its destiny and meaning are bound up with God. As his chosen race, his royal priesthood, his holy nation, it has been set apart to proclaim the wonderful acts of God who has called his people out of darkness into his marvellous light.[10] The Church is called to holiness. But it is a holiness which finds its authenticity and power not in withdrawal from the world, but through a costly identification and missionary engagement with the world in all its complexity, pain and potential. Yet the Church should remember that there was also a rhythm about the holiness of its Lord which it would do well to emulate, especially in these days of excessive activity. It was the rhythm of engagement, withdrawal, re-engagement. There is a time for work and there is a time for renewal and both are interrelated. If the Church is to grow in holiness it needs to get the balance right.

## Partnership renewed

If the concept of 'community as the bearer of mission'[11] is to have any credible content then it must also include renewal of that partnership which is not only crucial for mission but vital for the health of the Church. At this point I am not thinking about the great variety of partnerships, including those between rich and poor, black and white, young and old, male and female – all of which are important and need to be fostered within the Church. The partnership

I wish to emphasise, in relation to the concerns of this particular chapter, is the one between clergy and laity. Renewal in this particular partnership would not only release energy and vision within the Church, it would also transform its life and greatly facilitate its mission.

In the last twenty-five years great strides have been made in this partnership, resulting in the long overdue re-emergence of the laity. I use the word re-emergence because, of course, from the very beginning Protestant missions were, to a significant extent, a lay movement. The voluntary societies were not restricted to clerics. Though some clergy may have been involved in their founding, many of their most prominent members were lay people of substance and ability. Some such societies have been described as 'free, open, responsible, embracing all classes, both sexes, all ages, the masses of the people – a truly democratic and anti-authoritarian movement, to some extent anti-clerical and anti-establishment'.[12] Some of my lay school friends have just retired home from missionary service overseas, having founded churches, built hospitals and helped establish theological colleges. The history of lay ministry in the Church is in many cases a distinguished one, particularly in relation to the world Church.

On the home front, however, the Church has been far less adventurous. Thankfully there are signs of real vision and imagination in the developing partnership between clergy and laity. But signs are not realities. Like our worship and our community life this partnership also needs to be open to the Spirit in order that it may be transformed. Such transformation must be built on the basis of truth and trust.

## AWAY WITH STEREOTYPES

The Greek word *laos*, from which our word laity comes, refers to all the people of God. Though there may be a difference in function there is no difference in status amongst the people of God. In a strict etymological sense every member of the Church, ordained or non-ordained, is a member of the laity. The trouble usually comes when the clergy forget that they are laity, and the laity regret that they are laity.

In a recent visit to a group of laity I was encouraging them to play their full part in the life of their local church. I got a bit carried away with enthusiasm and exhorted them, in sporting parlance, 'to pick up the ball and run with it'. One fairly forthright character replied, 'My vicar won't let me have the ball and even if I did manage to get hold of it he would blow the whistle and stop me running with it.' Clearly there was no meaningful partnership between clergy and laity in that church. One of the partners was interested only in controlling the other.

But it isn't all one-sided. I went to preach at a harvest festival service in a rural church. The vicar was preaching elsewhere so I arrived early enough to familiarise myself with the situation. As soon as I opened the front door of the small church I was greeted by a friendly, smiling senior citizen. He extended his right hand to shake mine, while he continued to ring the church bell with his left. He directed me towards the vestry and said the churchwarden would be along in a moment. I found the vestry and had begun to robe when the bell stopped ringing. Thirty seconds later the door opened and in walked the erstwhile bellringer – who was also the churchwarden! He gave me some helpful guidance about the forthcoming service, reminding me, finally, to come to the rear of the church to pick up the choir before starting the service. With a smile he advised me not to begin the choir prayer until the bell stopped ringing. In due course I went to the choir vestry. There was no choir but, remembering my instructions, I waited until the bell stopped. The door of the choir vestry opened and in walked the erstwhile bellringer and church-warden – who had now become the choir. In solemn procession the two of us walked into church loudly singing 'We plough the fields and scatter the good seed on the land', and as we walked up the aisle, we passed forty other people among whom were men and women of great ability in the local community and in civic life. The story speaks for itself. If some clergy are, as they are often described, the cork in the bottle, then some laity fulfil the function of a screw-top.

## A POSITIVE APPROACH

Frankly, though we all have our horror stories to tell, I think the time has come to discard outdated and unhelpful stereotyping of clergy and laity over against each other. Besides, in ordaining clergy the bishops have only the laity to choose from! There really is a much more positive approach to the development of this crucial partnership and the biblical truth of the Holy Spirit's sovereignty in the distribution of his gifts is a key factor. There are four passages of scripture in the New Testament that speak of the gifts of God's Holy Spirit for ministry and mission.[13] Though they differ in emphasis there is one thing all have in common and that is their use of the word 'each'. Each member of the Body of Christ has been given his or her gifts to be used for the benefit of the whole. The Holy Spirit doesn't create omnicompetent ministers, only omni-competent congregations. He distributes his gifts to each and all of his people and the Church needs the contribution of all in order to fulfil God's purpose in ministry and mission. Given our mutual dependence on the same Holy Spirit, clergy and laity need to enter joyfully into partnership for mission in a spirit of mutual trust and respect.

The clergy don't wish to be overrated – and in this day and age it is increasingly unlikely – but they must not be underrated either. We really do not help matters by downplaying ordained ministry for, as Edward Schillebeeckx so pertinently remarked, 'If there is no specialized concentration of what is important to everyone, in the long run the community suffers as a result'.[14] In this connection I believe that ordained ministers serve as guardians, to help keep the community faithful to the teaching and practice of apostolic Christianity. Some are called and appointed to full-time ordained ministry in order that all may be reminded that discipleship is a lifetime calling. Lesslie Newbigin put the same truth another way, 'The priesthood of the ordained ministry is to enable, not to remove, the priesthood of the whole church.'[15]

But if the clergy are not to be underrated neither are the laity to be undervalued. Thankfully there is increasing evidence of laity being affirmed within the life of the Church and local congregation. As I move about the national church and across a large diocese it is heart-warming to witness the devotion, commitment and skill of so many lay people. I wanted to emphasise that positive point before going on to make what may be interpreted as a negative viewpoint – though I intend it to be quite the reverse. It concerns this whole question of the affirmation of the laity by the clergy and local church community. There is a tendency, and it may be encouraged by the laity themselves, to see such affirmation in terms of appointment to 'church-shaped' jobs. So, as well as readers and servers, we have pastoral auxiliaries, eucharistic assistants, music directors, and a host of new and imaginative roles for the laity to occupy – within the Church. I applaud all this. It is a wonderful indication of the growth in partnership between clergy and laity. But my basic and major concern is the one expressed so well in the report *All Are Called*: 'It is important for clergy and lay officials of the Church to recognise that the primary location of the laity is in society at large and only secondarily in the institutional church.'[16] God forbid that partnership should be aimed at turning laity into 'clergy clones'. 'Perish the thought' would be the reaction of most of us, yet so often the impression is given that we are doing just that. I frequently hear lay people complain that they are not being used or given appropriate work to do – in the Church. And my own experience as a minister in several different parishes is that there is often a hierarchy within the laity and it is determined by the nature of the 'church-shaped' jobs which people do.

All this has serious implications for mission. If an important part of mission is the reaching out in service to society in its need then, surely, the place to affirm, support and enable the laity is in that place where so much of their discipleship is formed and their contribution is so vital. There is much that the local clergy and the local church can do in order to be supportive and enabling of lay service in society, especially if they are prepared to listen carefully and respond imaginatively to what lay people say to them. But thinking lay people would be the first to admit that, just as the primary role of the laity is not to help the clergy do their job, but to fulfil their own discipleship in the Church and in society, so they must not expect the clergy to do their work for them. Richard Mouw's words are to the point: 'The clergy cannot do the laity's work for them, nor can the institutional church alone provide properly contextualised answers to the problems and dilemmas of the laity.'[17]

There is something immensely important here for the

whole question of renewal in partnership between clergy
and laity. Mouw's use of the term 'contextualised' is pertinent. Where you live and work helps to mould the way you
believe and the way you behave. The way you work out
your Christian discipleship is to some extent shaped by the
cultural, political and economic context by which you are
surrounded. If the Church is going to theologise about the
laity and develop a proper theology for lay ministry in
society, two things are important. The agenda must be set
by the needs, dilemmas and problems being encountered by
the laity. And the laity must be allowed and be willing to
bring their own experience of God, and of God in society,
into that discussion. It is vital to the ministry of the clergy
and to the mission of the Church that they do. 'If Christianity is not something existing apart from life, but the
transfiguration of life itself – and that means in the end
the transfiguration of the whole of life – it is to those who
are in the front line of the battle and are exposed to the
severest tests who are best able to teach us what Christianity
means as a living faith.'[18] Lay people are not by any means
minor partners. Their contribution is absolutely crucial,
but they have to be willing to offer it and the clergy and
the local church have to be ready and eager to accept it.
Thus will the corporate nature of the Church's calling be
emphasised and its vision for mission enlarged. David
Bosch, with a veiled reference to the return of the spies in
Numbers 13, sums up the nature of the partnership
superbly: 'Laypersons are no longer just the scouts, who,
returning from the "outside world" with eyewitness
accounts and perhaps some bunches of grapes, report to
the "operational basis"; they are the operational basis from
which the *missio Dei* proceeds. It is, in fact, not they who
have to "accompany" those who hold "special offices" in
the latter's mission in the world. Rather, it is the office
bearers who have to accompany the laity, the people of

God. In the New Testament dispensation the Spirit (just as the priesthood) has been given to the whole people of God, not to select individuals.'[19]

It is in openness to that Spirit that the Church will experience renewal for mission. The renewing Spirit will help transform our worshipping and community life and create that mutual trust in partnership between clergy and laity which is so vital.

## Open to God and the world

I want to conclude this chapter by returning to the four words with which the second paragraph began, in order to make two brief, but important, comments. The statement that 'Mission begins with prayer' served to direct our minds to the truth that the mission was God's and not ours. It is a truth we must never forget. All too easily prayer can be set aside as we begin to rely on strategy and statistics, numbers and success. These things are important and must not be despised, but without the undergirding and power of prayer mission will soon be perceived as ours and not God's. That would be a tragedy both for the Church and the world. It would mean that the Church had ceased to be God's servant and instead had become an independent company. In doing so it would have forgotten that it is not the Church which 'undertakes' mission; it is God's mission which constitutes the Church. 'Lord, teach us to pray' is a petition which the Church needs to use in every age.[20]

The second point is also with reference to those four words and concerns the work of the Holy Spirit in the world. Prayer, I stressed, was a reaching out towards God, an opening up of ourselves to him. But God is not confined to the Church. The Holy Spirit is not held hostage by the

Church. The mission of God constitutes the Church but is not contained by it. God through his Spirit is alive and active in his world, sometimes in co-operation with the Church and sometimes apart from it. For instance, in the human tragedies so frequently portrayed in such horrendous detail on our television screens, from places like Bosnia and Rwanda, Christian and non-Christian work side by side in offering humanitarian aid. Some of the most moving practical responses to the tragedy in Romania, the effects of which are still with us, came from those who did not claim to be members of the Church. Can any of us doubt, however, that the mission of God was being fulfilled through their life-transforming service to those in need? We will take this matter further in the next chapter. But perhaps some words of Bishop John V. Taylor will help us to keep our feet on the ground while, in seeking to be renewed for mission, we open ourselves to God's Spirit and God's world. 'The chief actor in the historic mission of the Christian Church is the Holy Spirit. He is the director of the whole enterprise. The mission consists of the things he is doing in the world.'[21]

## Study session

OPENING PRAYER

Spirit of the living God
Help us to discern not just what we should do,
But what kind of people you would have us be.

READING

Ephesians 4:1–16.

MEDITATIONS

'The Church, as an agent of mission, must itself be an example of God's transforming work.' (p. 26)

'The first call upon the Church and the individual Christian . . . is to worship God.' (p. 26)

'A Church which is open to God's Spirit is likely to reveal in its life a new concentration on Jesus Christ.' (p. 30)

'Christians are not meant to journey alone. Faith flourishes most when it exists within community.' (p. 32)

'Our world cries out for people who have learned how to forgive one another and how to settle wrongs and not be consumed with enmity and bitterness.' (p. 35)

'The Holy Spirit is not held hostage by the Church. The mission of God constitutes the Church but is not contained by it.' (pp. 44–45)

OUR EXPERIENCE

• Why do we worship together? What do you value most about being part of a worshipping community?

• 'The Holy Spirit doesn't create omnicompetent ministers, only omnicompetent congregations.' (p. 40) How and why?

• In what sense do you experience the Church as community? What values, commitments and actions express this most in your context (either at present or as an ideal)?

CHRISTIAN RESPONSE

• What power has this liturgy to change the lives of those who name the name of Christ? What is life-transforming about this worship that would send this community out to be agents of transformation in society? What have we discovered about God which simply must be shared with the world around? (p. 28)

• Divide into three groups to consider your church's worshipping life through the lens of the three questions above. Compare your answers. What clues emerge for the renewal of your church as a worshipping community?

• 'The ideal and the actual community belong together.' (p. 33) Give everyone in the group a piece of paper with a 'dream balloon' drawn on it. Ask them to write or draw something to express how they would like their Christian community life to be in five years' time. What would the Church look and feel like? Pool your ideas. What kind of people must we become to make the dream a reality? (pp. 33–37)

• 'Trouble usually comes when the clergy forget that they are laity, and the laity regret that they are laity.' (pp. 39ff.) What simple description of the distinctive but complementary roles of clergy and laity would liberate both them and the Church for more effective collaboration? (pp. 39–44)

ACTION

• Devise a congregational survey and follow-up discussion on prayer and worship, the renewal of Christian community or clergy–lay collaboration.

• Use this to shape decisions by the church council.

CLOSING PRAYER

God of love and renewal,
Inspire our worship and service,
Enlarge our sense of community
    and, by your Spirit,
Unite and empower us for the work of mission.

# 3

# Mission and the Kingdom

Exploring the call to seek the Kingdom
as part of the mission of God

'Why are we getting side-tracked by all this "guff" about social responsibility? That's not the Church's task. Why can't we concentrate on preaching the gospel?' That was the sad and rather frightening comment heard at a recent meeting of a deanery synod which was discussing mission. It was sad because it revealed that the speaker had been equipped with the proverbial blinkers and ear plugs. He had shown himself to be blind and deaf to the honest arguments, shared experiences, perceptive comments and personal stories of those who surrounded him that evening. But it was also somewhat frightening. It portrayed a local church leader who had misunderstood or failed to comprehend the very nature of the gospel he wanted to hear preached. Even worse, perhaps, it was an indication that the context of that preaching was being totally ignored.

Jesus didn't preach the gospel in a vacuum. There was a specific context into which he came and to which he spoke. If we are to follow his call to mission with any kind of integrity we cannot ignore the context in which we serve and the nature and content of the gospel we are called to proclaim.

In this chapter we shall address some of the questions raised by this comment at the deanery synod: What is the gospel? What is the relationship between the gospel and the mission of God's Kingdom? How does Jesus' own life and teaching open up for us a way of understanding how these relate together? And what does all this mean for the Church?

We will begin with some words from Jesus himself. What did Jesus mean by the gospel? What are we meant to understand by it? The fact that thousands of books have been written on the subject may be an indication that the meaning of the gospel is not as obvious as we sometimes suppose. But at least we know what the message of the gospel was. At the very beginning of his ministry Jesus said, 'The time has come. The Kingdom of God is near. Repent and believe the good news.' (Mark 1:15). If we are looking for the keynote of the faith of Jesus of Nazareth, this is it. It was the proclamation of this message that moved people so powerfully. The proclamation by Jesus of the proximity of the Kingdom and his brief public ministry that accompanied it have been called 'an "explosion of energy" without parallel in recorded history'.[1]

In his Sermon on the Mount Jesus exhorted us to 'Seek first the kingdom of God and his righteousness' (Matthew 6:33). Dr John Stott says of these words that they 'embrace our Christian evangelistic and social responsibilities. In order to seek first God's kingdom we must evangelise, since the kingdom spreads only as the gospel is preached, heard, believed and obeyed. In order to seek first God's righteousness we shall still evangelise, but we shall also engage in social action and endeavour to spread throughout the community those higher standards of righteousness which are pleasing to God.'[2] Jesus practised what he preached. There was no false dichotomy between preaching the gospel and social responsibility. His prophetic ministry was described as powerful in both word and deed and many of his parables, such as those of the unforgiving servant and the

Good Samaritan, called for a revolutionary righteouness (right living and right dealing) in terms of social action.[3]

Certainly, if we are going to engage in mission, and at the same time understand the meaning of the gospel we are called to proclaim, we will need to come to terms, as far as it is possible to do so, with the nature and reality of the Kingdom of God as taught in the scriptures.

## What on earth is 'the Kingdom of God'?

The concept of the Kingdom of God did not begin with Jesus. It had developed over a long period of Israel's history. When Jesus began his public ministry by announcing that with his coming the Kingdom of God was drawing near, he did so on the assumption that the idea was already familiar to his listeners. For us in the twentieth century the concept carries difficult overtones of monarchy, riches, distance and power, and unhappy associations with over-bearing male dominance. As we shall see, the Kingdom values as taught by Jesus turned these values upside down.

The Aramaic words that he almost certainly used meant, literally, 'the kingdom of the heavens'. The term 'the heavens' was one of those phrases which Jews tended to employ in order to avoid using the sacred name of God. So, Matthew, because of his Jewish-Christian background, makes use of the vernacular 'Kingdom of Heaven', whereas Mark and Luke give the actual meaning of the phrase, namely, the 'Kingdom (or reign) of God'. But whatever phrase was used it resonated with a longing within the consciousness of Israel.

Outstanding in the historical memory of the people of Israel was the experience of the Exodus, the rescue of the Israelites from years as slaves in Egypt. 'I am the Lord your

God who brought you out of the land of Egypt' (Exodus 20:2). This famous rescue story became one of the most powerful symbols not only for Israel but for oppressed people throughout the ages. It was a story frequently on the lips of Martin Luther King in his struggle for human rights and it certainly formed a major part of the persuasive and prophetic preaching of Archbishop Desmond Tutu in the struggle for freedom in South Africa. It is the story central to the Liberation Theology of Latin America.

The experience of Exodus and the subsequent linking of God's life and will with her fortunes convinced Israel that God was not only on her side but also that he was the 'one God' who ruled or reigned over all. The eventual failure of human institutions such as monarchy and priesthood only served to focus Israel's attention on the future vindication of her hopes by a further intervention by God to establish his rule or reign. Examples of this can be seen in the references to the kingly figure of the Messiah in early Isaiah: 'Your eyes will see the king in his beauty . . . the Lord is our king, it is he who will save us'.[4]


NARROW OR COMPREHENSIVE?


While Jesus did not invent the concept of the Kingdom of God he certainly transformed it, giving it new content and meaning. It was within that context of somewhat distant expectation that Jesus made his dramatic announcement that with his arrival on the scene the Kingdom had drawn near and required, indeed demanded, an immediate response and a radical change – 'turn around and believe the gospel'. No longer could it be thought of only in terms of future and distant events. It had drawn near, indeed with his coming it was knocking at the very gates.

Given the sense of urgency contained in his announce-

ment of the Kingdom and the frequent occurrence of the
phrase in the synoptic gospels (ninety-eight times as compared with only twenty-four times in the rest of the New
Testament) it may seem surprising that we are never told
in so many words what it is. We shall search the scriptures in vain for a definition of the Kingdom of God. Life
might have been easier if we had been told, but I doubt it.
Definitions have a tendency to exclude, often in an arbitrary
manner, people and things which don't quite fit. That,
perhaps above all else, would be false to the picture of the
Kingdom portrayed in the scriptures and particularly in
the life and ministry of Jesus.

Because the meaning of the Kingdom is not spelled out,
what Jesus meant by it can only be deduced by the things
he said, the way he lived his life and the priorities he set
for his ministry. The picture he presented of a gracious
God, his insistence on mixing with outcasts, his healing
and exorcisms, his conflicts over the interpretation of law,
all helped to form, as we shall see, a cumulative and comprehensive definition of what he meant by the Kingdom of
God – a comprehensiveness which was underlined by his
teaching in parables, most, if not all, of which describe
some aspect of the Kingdom of God.

## The Kingdom and mission

It is this comprehensiveness as perceived in the words and
works of Jesus that is so important for our understanding
of mission. The balance and integration he achieved
between word and action, as instanced in the Sermon on
the Mount, is a model for us to follow. A failure to understand this can lead to the kind of remark made at that
deanery synod discussion on mission and to the barren

debates about mission versus evangelism which, in my experience, generate more heat than light.

The concerns of mission cannot be any less comprehensive and fluid than the concerns of the Kingdom. This may be the reason why Jesus deliberately chose the theme of the Kingdom as the most appropriate way of expressing and explaining the meaning and scope of his mission.

The character of the Kingdom, out of which was formed the interpretation of his mission, appeared to have three dimensions. First, Israel's hopes and ultimate destiny were bound up with it – so much so that when Jesus made his dramatic announcement that with his arrival the Kingdom had come close, he was in reality claiming that his mission was inseparably linked with Israel's history. The decisive moment in that history had come. Secondly, in the Old Testament the coming of the Kingdom was synonymous with the coming of God. It was God's presence for which the people looked and longed. That's why the term 'kingdom' is translated by many as 'the reign of God'. It may also account for the prominence that Jesus gave to his teaching about the nature of God. Thirdly, the Kingdom, unmistakably, had a saving character. At the Exodus God had saved and delivered his people. As we have seen, that experience proved formative in the history of Israel. The God who is coming to reign is one who has already shown himself to be committed to saving his people. The kingly clothing of the Messiah figure in the early chapters of Isaiah are replaced by those of 'the Servant' in the second part of Isaiah. That deliverance will include the destruction of pain, sickness, evil and death – aspects of the rule of God clearly displayed in the life and mission of Jesus.

## A REVEALING RELATIONSHIP

But at the heart of the mission of Jesus, and of his revelation of the nature of the Kingdom, was his relationship with God. It was from that remarkably free and intimate relationship that there emerged a view of the Kingdom and of mission that was strikingly comprehensive. One word above all others sums up the relationship. It is the word 'abba'. It is an expression of intimacy, an Aramaic and rather homely word by which a child addressed his father. There may be many reasons why Jesus was able to engage with such intimacy with God, including, of course, 'the glory which he had with his Father before the world began' (John 17:5). But, surely, there is one very obvious reason, namely, that Jesus had experienced God as gracious, loving, merciful and compassionate. The awesome God of Israel is a loving father of incredible compassion: a father who is concerned for, and immediately responsive to, the needs of his children.

Parable after parable reinforces this insight into the nature of God. In the stories of the lost sheep, the lost coin and the lost son, for instance, it is the extravagant generosity of God in pursuing even one of his wayward children that holds centre stage.[5] It is this same generosity, taken almost beyond the bounds of fairness, that people begrudged in the parable of the workers hired at the eleventh hour.[6] God's compassion is unconditional, 'he causes his sun to rise on the evil and the good and sends rain on the righteous and the unrighteous' (Matthew 5:45).

## GENEROSITY BEYOND BELIEF

It is this generous and indiscriminate compassion on the part of God that puts the demands of the Kingdom and the call for response to the gospel into perspective. Here is no powerful potentate calling for obedience, or else! Here is a loving father who wants his children to discover the treasure that can be theirs through the gift of his grace and mercy. One of the marks of good kingship was concern for the well-being (*shalom*) of the people. The amazing compassion of God calls for a response. The call to repent, or turn around, is an essential element in the Kingdom concept: 'The kingdom of God is near. Repent and believe the good news.' God's overwhelming compassion is not cheap grace but transforming grace. I don't suppose there has been a more striking modern demonstration of this than that displayed by Gordon Wilson in the wake of the infamous Enniskillen, Remembrance Day, massacre. As he held the broken body of his beloved daughter in his arms, his words, directed at the terrorists, were free from bitterness and cries for revenge. Instead there is an amazing compassion that prays for his enemies, that expresses forgiveness, that calls for reconciliation. Here also was no cheap grace but a grace that transformed him and many of his enemies also. When the full story is told of the troubles in Northern Ireland I hope that due attention will be paid to the transforming compassion and grace of God revealed in and through the lives of ordinary people. To 'seek the Kingdom' is a commitment to share in God's generosity.

BEYOND THE PALE

But if one aspect of the Kingdom and therefore of mission is God's overwhelming compassion as revealed in Jesus, then an equally astonishing aspect is his outrageous association with the dregs of society. He went to parties with sinners. He made friends with those whom others despised. His sympathies were for the poor and defenceless. He stood on the side of the oppressed against the oppressors. He was prepared to ignore religious prohibitions, choosing, for example, not only to mix with women, but also to include them among his community of followers and to accept their affection and loyalty.

Such behaviour on the part of a religious teacher was considered scandalous. But it was the outcome of his special relationship with God. It was the compelling compassion of the God of the Kingdom that sent him in mission across man-made barriers towards the outcast and the sinner. By his teaching, his life and his actions he not only mirrored the true prophetic tradition, he also made a clear statement about the nature of the God who was coming to reign and to transform: a God who was not prepared to be imprisoned within convention or even, it would seem, within religion; a God who was free to cross racial and cultural boundaries; a God who could be recklessly generous and outrageously merciful.

These same characteristics of God and the Kingdom are also evident in our Lord's attitude to certain elements in the law. Jesus was a loyal Jew but in the interests of compassion he was prepared to enter into conflict with his opponents because of their narrow and insensitive interpretation of the law.[7] By word and deed he indicated that law was subordinate to love when it came to addressing human need. Indeed, the law was intended to give guidance in loving. Thus Jesus demonstrated that the reign of 'the coming God' was geared towards nourishing rather than crushing human life.

He also demonstrated that such a rule would be directed towards deliverance from pain, sickness, evil and death. As we noted above, the concept of the Kingdom which Jesus inherited included a saving element. His announcement declared that it had drawn near. His actions proved the validity of his words. He healed the sick, he released people

from a whole variety of psychological afflictions, he cast
out evil spirits and he declared that such activity was related
to the Kingdom of God: 'If I drive out demons by the
finger of God, then the kingdom of God has come to you.'
(Luke 11:20)

What seems to emerge, therefore, from the life and teaching of Jesus is a picture of the Kingdom which cannot be
narrowed down to one particular aspect. It is universal in
its application. 'It embraces all: the world, the human
person, and society; the totality of reality is to be transformed by God.'[8] 'God's Kingdom is creation healed.'[9] But
that is not only a portrayal of the Kingdom of God, it is
also a picture of the extent of God's transforming mission.

So while we must be careful lest in designating everything
as mission we divest the term of its meaning we also need
to guard against dragging mission into such narrow confines
that it simply becomes the expression of our own predilections or, dare I say it, prejudices. 'Mission describes everything the church is sent into the world to do.'[10] (It does not
describe everything the Church does – such as worship and
nurture – and God is at work beyond the Church.)

So far in this chapter we have probed the meaning of the
Kingdom of God and its relationship to the mission of
God. In doing so we have been helped by some insights
into the nature of that God whose Kingdom and mission
it is. All these things that we have been exploring come
together in the person of Jesus in whom the Kingdom of
God is embodied, made visible and lived out.


## The Kingdom and the Lord

One of the noticeable differences between the Gospels and
the other sections of the New Testament is that in the

Gospels the focus is on the coming Kingdom, but in the rest of the New Testament the focus is on Jesus as the one who fleshes out the very being of God. This is why the phrase 'Jesus is Lord' became the primary creed in the Early Church. There is no inconsistency here. The Kingdom and the King go together. Some of the parables, such as the Parable of the Wedding Banquet, make this explicit.[11] As we have already seen, the Kingdom of God means the reign of God, and the shape of that reign is Christ. His 'lordship', or rule, picks up those aspects of the nature of God that formed the very heart of the good news. But he turned the traditional ideas of lordship upside down, giving a dramatic demonstration of its meaning and content on the floor of the upper room when he washed the feet of his disciples.[12] He presents a picture of 'the Servant King'. There is no overbearing or domineering authority here. He refuses to drive people, preferring to lead them by example. And by that example he teaches that God's reign is by invitation and attraction, not by force.

It is with that understanding that we must follow Paul's example in proclaiming 'Jesus as Lord', not with an arrogant and insensitive triumphalism but with a true humility of spirit which not only matches the nature of his lordship but which also attracts rather than repels. But that does not detract from the powerful implications of the claim which, besides being mind-blowing, set an incredible agenda for mission. To my mind, no one demonstrated this more effectively than Bishop Lesslie Newbigin when he wrote, the 'affirmation that "Jesus is Lord", implied a commitment to make good that confession in relation to the whole life of the world – its philosophy, its culture and its politics no less than the personal lives of its people. The Christian mission is the acting out in the whole life of the whole world of the confession that Jesus Christ is Lord of all.'[13]

The vision emanating from the confession of Jesus Christ

as Lord is large enough and challenging enough to occupy
the Church in its missionary task until the Kingdom comes
in its ultimate fullness. The splendour of the vision catches
us up into itself and allows us the enormous privilege of
sharing in the mission task.

## Our lives a prayer

At the inaugural service which marked the beginning of
my episcopal ministry in the Diocese of Southwark I felt
constrained to preach on the theme of seeking the Kingdom. The Church of England at that particular time was,
it seemed, circumscribed by controversies about its own life
and ministry. The ordination of women to the priesthood
appeared to dominate every discussion. The agenda of the
Church was consumed by debates, often cantankerous,
about ministry. During that period I found some words of
John Robinson, a former Bishop of Woolwich, both liberat-
ing and challenging, so much so that I quoted them in my
sermon. He wrote, 'Just as the New Testament bids us have
as high a doctrine of the ministry as we like, as long as our
doctrine of the Church is higher, so it commands us to
have as high a doctrine of the Church as we may, provided
our doctrine of the Kingdom is higher.'[14] The words struck
the right note for me. They endorsed the emphasis I felt
constrained to make in lifting the eyes of the Anglican
Church in Southwark over and beyond its immediate and
legitimate concerns towards the wider context and concerns
of the Kingdom of God. I was convinced that the larger
vision of 'The Rule of God' in our lives, our Church, our
communities, the life of the earth and the whole of creation,
was to be the motivation behind our mission.

It was while preparing for that sermon that I came across

a little phrase in the Canadian Prayer Book. It formed part of the prayer at the end of Psalm 141 and read, 'that our lives may be a prayer for the coming of your kingdom'. At the time, the phrase struck me like a bolt of lightning. It was a call to consistency between my actions and my aspirations. I pray daily in the words of the Lord's prayer for the coming of the Kingdom but I must also become part of the answer to my prayer by basing my life on Kingdom values and Kingdom standards. Here is a truth, blindingly obvious but so often ignored, that enables every individual to be involved in mission, in the work of transforming society. My life and yours are not insignificant in that larger scheme of things. If the marks of the Kingdom, the reign of God, are discernible and developing in your life and mine, it is not only a contribution towards the coming of the Kingdom, it is a sharing in the transforming mission of God. If we are committed to peace-making within the community, to justice in all our affairs, to right living and dealing in all our relationships, we both manifest the Kingdom and mirror the characteristics of the King. We give substance to the confession that Jesus is Lord and, we hope, avoid the inconsistency challenged by Jesus in his words, 'Why do you call me, Lord, Lord, and do not do what I say?' (Luke 6:46). But, even more than that, if we are being brought to the Kingdom of his glory (shalom, righteousness, justice, and so on) we must form our lives and societies now in the light of it – 'Thy kingdom come on earth as it is in heaven'. In other words, the Kingdom to which we are being drawn requires us to behave in certain compatible ways now.

We will also demonstrate that mission is not always 'church shaped'. Most of our life is spent in a non-church environment. Lambeth 1988 made this point well: 'the primary ministry of the great majority of Christians is their service of humanity in the everyday work of the world'.[15]

Living the Kingdom in such circumstances will not always be discerned or interpreted as doing the 'church' thing. Indeed, in issues of peace, justice and right dealing, we may be joined by the most improbable companions. This should not surprise us for it is not we who extend the Kingdom of God. That is God's task and his alone. Our task is to announce it, to receive it and, by the way we live, reveal its values and standards. God is free and able to extend his Kingdom in the most unlikely places through the most unlikely people.

At the heart of our initiation services is the call for the new Christian to be allied to Christ in the cause of the Kingdom. We say to those about to be baptised or confirmed, 'You must with your own mouth and from your own heart declare your allegiance to Christ *and* your rejection of all that is evil.' Many of our friends and acquaintances would not be able to join with us in the first of these two requirements but they would stand shoulder to shoulder with us in the second. Day after day in hospitals, schools, factories and offices, in the world of medicine, education, technology and commerce, the Kingdom draws near. Wherever injustice is opposed, racism is rebuked, ignorance is dispelled, healing is experienced, and reconciliation takes place, there the frontiers of evil are driven back, the Kingdom comes and the transforming mission of God proceeds on its way. Jesus is Lord of all. His sovereignty and his continuing work through his Spirit are not limited to his Church.

## The Church a sign

The Church of God and the Kingdom of God are not synonymous though, in the eyes of some, they may be

mistakenly identified. Nevertheless there is an intimate connection between them and the mission of the Church is
closely linked with the Kingdom. The Church is a sign of
the Kingdom. It is not in the world for its own sake but
for the salvation of the world. 'It has no ends but those of
the Kingdom of God.'[16] It proclaims the coming of the
Kingdom in Jesus Christ and, as a community of grace,
anticipates the coming of the final Kingdom. Its task is to
hold the values and standards of the Kingdom, however
imperfectly, for the whole of society. God's ultimate purpose is for the transformation of human society in terms of
a new heaven and a new earth. In the light of this the
Church has a preparatory role by witnessing to the transforming power of God in its own life. It has been said that
the Church is in the business of inventing the future, that is,
of revealing in the present moment something of God's
ultimate purpose for his creation. Perhaps, at its simplest,
the Church is called to embody the Kingdom, to put flesh
on Kingdom values, standards and priorities. Such a task
is vital to its mission, both at local and national level.

AT THE LOCAL LEVEL

One of the challenges facing the Church at the local level,
therefore, is to display in its own life the Rule of God which
it proclaims to others. Given that Jesus manifested by his
words and deeds the characteristics of the Kingdom, how
far do those characteristics determine the priorities of the
local church? A searching test for any church council or
church committee seeking to assess its present work and
plan its future strategy would be to discern how effective
the local church is as a sign of the Kingdom. A healthy
bank balance, a large membership, a superb choir and a
fine building are all things for which we may wish to thank

God but they are not necessarily signs of the Kingdom. Nor, for that matter, is a small congregation with a large overdraft and an inferior building! Perhaps a more enlightened enquiry would include the following: Are poor people welcomed and empowered? Are they encouraged to participate fully in the life of the congregation, including the decision-making process? Does the local community see our church as an open, healing, compassionate community? Just how easy or how difficult is it for people to feel they 'belong'? Is the Church confronting injustice and actively promoting the well-being of all within the local community? Though it may be a painful process, answers to such questions need to be sought from those 'outside' the Church and not just from those who are on the inside and claim to be 'members'!

### AT THE NATIONAL LEVEL

The Church is also called to be a sign of the Kingdom at national level. Inevitably this will involve the Church in confronting a remarkable, and somewhat naive, national 'double-think'. The Church is called to 'give a moral lead' and, at the same time, 'to keep out of politics'. The latter exhortation continues to be heard despite the fact that very many devout and committed Christians, and people of other faiths, serve out their vocation within the world of politics.

When I was Bishop of Bradford, I dared to 'interfere' in that world of politics by publicly opposing City Council decisions to introduce massive financial cuts that would seriously affect the poorest members of the community. As a result I was subjected to a considerable barrage of criticism. This negative reaction was not so much focused on the meat of the matter, namely, injustice and the plight of the poor, but on the fact that I had had the temerity to tread where angels feared to tread. Political debate of such a nitty-gritty, and at times very rigorous, kind was considered 'not quite the thing' for a bishop to be engaged in. I have to record that good politicians did not take this narrow view. They welcomed it as a proper contribution towards the formation of good policy.

When Shirley Williams entitled her book *Politics is for people*, she was really echoing the Deuteronomists. In the Old Testament the law was given 'that you may live, and that it may go well with you' (Deuteronomy 5:33, RSV). The law belongs within the covenant of grace, the calling to the people to live in relationship with God, where their welfare, or *shalom*, is found. The Old Testament law is summarised in the commands to love God and love neighbour and endorsed as such by Jesus and by St Paul. God's law, in other words, reflects the character of God, and demonstrates a pattern of life appropriate for human beings made in God's image. The social and political expression of neighbour love is justice – and that relates as much to social systems as to personal values.

So the Church, if it is to fulfil its role as a sign of the Kingdom, has an inescapable interest in politics and in social morality because of its interest in human well-being, and in the social cohesion within which human beings can flourish. St Paul's view of government, illustrated in Romans 13, indicates that 'the powers that be' have a limited and temporary, but none the less God-given, role in providing a context in which justice can be sustained and evil curbed. Part of the role of the Church, as a sign of the Kingdom, is to remind governments of their God-given responsibilities and that they are accountable to him.

There are aspects of our social and economic systems where it is entirely right for the Church to 'interfere'. Where power in public life is abused to the detriment of others and where injustice is perpetrated through our social systems, the Church cannot stand aloof and silent. It has a duty to stand up and be counted. It has an obligation to promote those values for human well-being and social justice which are enshrined in its foundation documents. The Church is not called to wave moral banners. It is not in the business of legalism. But it is called to be a sign of the Kingdom and, itself, to seek for the application of Kingdom values and standards within its own life. And, because it believes that such values as justice, righteousness and peace are crucial to the true well-being of all people, it must actively pursue such values in the whole life of the whole nation.

PHYSICIAN HEAL YOURSELF

However, 'judgement must begin with the family of God' (1 Peter 4:17). If the Church is to pursue and maintain an effective and radical mission towards the nation, seeking the nation's true health and wholeness through a prophetic ministry of the Word of God, it must also open itself to the necessity for radical repentance, reform and renewal. It is not without significance that prophets like Amos directed their strongest words to the people of God. In Israel in the eighth century BC, he denounced the growing gap between rich and poor and underlined the powerlessness of poverty. He criticised the immorality in social leaders, recognised that social institutions were promoting injustice and that even religious institutions had become hijacked for political ends. He believed that God is sovereign Lord of all, that human beings are precious to God, and called for justice to 'roll down like waters, and righteousness like an everflowing stream' (Amos 5:24, RSV).

There are those who believe that until the Church itself

is free from fault it cannot be an effective sign of the Kingdom. I cannot submit to such a view. One of the reasons
why I believe that the report *Faith in the City* proved so
powerful an influence was its recognition that the Church
as well as the nation had failed to address seriously the
scandal of urban deprivation and decay. The Church admit-
ted that it needed to put its own house in order, and
proceeded to do so. Its challenge to the nation, therefore,
was all the more powerful.

In practical terms, as a prophet, Amos was a failure.
Samaria soon fell; but he stood in the breach and bore
witness to God's purpose for humanity. There are those
who would write off the Church as irrelevant and a failure.
But, in the economy and Kingdom of God failure and
weakness are neither despised nor dismissed. With God
weakness can prove stronger than power.

THAT OUR LIES MAY BE A PRAYER?

Soon after I discovered that formative phrase, 'that our lives
may be a prayer for the coming of the Kingdom', I shared
it with an American friend, telling him that I intended to
use it in my enthronement sermon. He became excited
about it, describing it as a most unusual and apt idea. To
be honest, I was a little surprised at his response which
seemed rather 'over the top'. Then I discovered that a
combination of his ageing ears and my Ulster accent made
him think that I had said, 'that our *lies* may be a prayer for
the coming of the kingdom'! But, on reflection, isn't that
too what we want both for ourselves and for the Church as
a sign of the Kingdom? Are we not only too well aware of
the great gap that so often exists between what we profess
to be and what we actually are? But, perhaps, God can take
even what we pretend to be and, in some mysterious way,

use even our untruth for his glory. And, of course, this does happen, or where would any of us be today? St Paul, I believe, would underline that particular point. Indeed, his experience is a clear illustration of how all the moral righteousness and rectitude that his position and breeding gave him counted as nothing. In fact it was a lie, when compared to the righteousness that he found in Christ. But somehow, his zeal and commitment, although misguided, was turned into a prayer for the Kingdom, once he had been confronted by the overwhelming love and grace of God.

The fact is that the Church must live with contradiction. In that sense the Church is always in crisis, caught in the tension between its essential nature and its empirical condition, between what it is and what it is called to be. But that should neither deflect it from its missionary task nor distract it from its call to be a sign of the Kingdom. On the contrary, it should be a motivating factor on both counts. The pursuit of Kingdom values in society must be matched by a pursuit of Kingdom values in the Church. They go hand in hand. That was what the 1988 Lambeth Conference had in mind when it said:

> We see signs of the Kingdom's presence:
> when men and women, being justified by faith, become a new creation in Christ;
> when women and men are being healed at their deepest spiritual, physical and emotional levels;
> when the poor are no longer hungry and are treated justly as God's beloved;
> when the church takes seriously the formation of women and men in the likeness of Christ through the work of the Holy Spirit;
> when unjust structures of society are changed into structures of grace.[17]

A closer look at that statement from the Lambeth Conference may give us a clue as to why the Church is seen by some to be a curiosity and by others to be a threat. It may also account for the 'double-think' that calls upon the Church to give a moral lead and, at the same time, to keep out of politics. 'Saving souls' is something which society is prepared to delegate to the Church. Such a task is considered slightly old-fashioned, rather curious and somewhat irrelevant in a modern technological age. But, if it must, let the Church get on with it. It can't do much harm and it may do a bit of good for people who 'need that sort of thing'. People being 'healed at their deepest spiritual, physical and emotional level' seems a good idea!

However, when we come to the changing of unjust structures into structures of grace, that's a different matter. The Church is no longer seen as a curiosity, shunted into a privatised siding for those who are 'into religion'. Instead it is perceived as a threat by those who have a vested interest in maintaining structures that are patently unjust and to the disadvantage of the poor.

Some would say, in such matters, the Church should mind its own business. It should stick to spiritual and moral matters and leave the shaping of society to those whose task it is. But for the Church to follow such advice or bow to such criticism would be to deny its missionary charter and to opt out of its responsibility to be a sign and forerunner of the Kingdom of God.

We have noted earlier that the people of God in the Old Testament were energised by their memory of the Exodus. They saw it as crucial to their life and destiny. It kept them hopeful in days of darkness and captivity. Later on, when the monarchy was in disarray, they would look back to the Exodus as a source of hope that God would not abandon

them, a hope that expected a coming King. Similarly, the
Church is a community 'rooted in energized memories and
summoned by radical hopes'.[18] No wonder, therefore, that
the Church is seen as either a curiosity or a threat. What
else could it be in the midst of a consumer society character-
ised by a depreciation of memory and a ridicule of hope –
a society in which the present moment is all important?

Of course, the central heart of the Christian gospel is
seen in all its fullness in the death and Resurrection of
Jesus. We will look more fully at the Cross and the empty
tomb in Chapter 5, but for now simply note that the
memory of the Cross and the Resurrection energises the
Church's mission. The Resurrection not only declared Jesus
to be both Lord and Christ, it also proclaimed that there
was grace beyond regret and hope beyond failure. The
central theme, therefore, of our missionary message is that
Christ is risen. And, consequently, the Church is called to
live the Resurrection life in the here and now, and be a sign
of contradiction against the forces of death and destruction.
Through the risen Christ the Church is both rooted in
energised memories and summoned by radical hopes.
Transformation is not only at the heart of the meaning of
the Resurrection, it also sums up the aim of mission and the
purpose of the Kingdom.

## Living tomorrow's life today

The Kingdom in the teaching of Jesus was 'not yet'. But it
was so close that the only proper response was to anticipate
its arrival and begin to live the future now. This is not as
sophisticated as it may sound. And there are illustrations
of it all around us. The Columbanus Community in Belfast,
for instance, which I mentioned in Chapter 2, has been

living the future for two decades. Confronted by the poison
of sectarianism that has seeped into every part of life in
Northern Ireland, threatening to destroy it, that small,
seemingly insignificant community of Catholics and Protestants has been living, praying and serving together. In
other words they have been living the future, bringing into
the present the reconciliation and peace for which they have
been praying and working and longing. Their lives have not
only been a prayer for the coming of the Kingdom of justice
and peace, their community has been a sign of that Kingdom. Against all the odds they have been living tomorrow's
life today.

I believe that is the urgent task to which the Church is
called. Of course, it seems absurd to enter into the 'not
yet' now. But then the Kingdom is full of absurdities. In it
the values and standards of the world are turned upside-
down. To seek the Kingdom is to be open to the rule of
God in our lives, our Church, our communities, the life
of the earth and the whole of creation. We begin to live
tomorrow's life today when we have the audacity and bold-
ness to place ourselves under God's control and live out
the implications of his rule in a society that refuses to
submit to his sovereignty.

It's a tall order, a demanding challenge. Nevertheless
such a commitment lies at the heart of God's mission
through his Church. A Church committed to mission must
proclaim Jesus as Lord. But it must also, in every aspect of
its life, practise what it preaches. This is what that deanery
synod member did not seem to appreciate. It must reveal
compassion and generosity for that is in keeping with the
nature of God. It must confront injustice of every kind for
that is in line with the will of God. It must humbly accept
the rule of God, for that is the essence of the Kingdom
and the basis for mission. The prophet summed it up in a
nutshell when he said:

He has showed you, O man, what is good.
And what does the Lord require of you?
To act justly and to love mercy
and to walk humbly with your God.

(Micah 6:8)

## Study session

OPENING PRAYER

Sovereign God,
Give us hearts attuned to the presence
of your kingdom in our midst
through our world
and beyond our wildest imagining.

READINGS

Isaiah 33:17, 22; Matthew 6:33.

MEDITATIONS

'The amazing compassion of God calls for a response . . .
It is not cheap grace but transforming grace.' (p. 56)

'God's Kingdom is creation healed.' (p. 58)

'The Kingdom of God means the reign of God, and the
shape of that reign is Christ.' (p. 59)

'If we are committed to peace-making within the community, to justice in all our affairs, to right living and dealing in all our relationships, we both manifest the Kingdom and mirror the characteristics of the King.' (p. 61)

'The Church is a sign of the Kingdom. It is not in the world for its own sake but for the salvation of the world.' (p. 63)

'The Kingdom is full of absurdities. In it the values and standards of the world are turned upside-down.' (p. 71)

OUR EXPERIENCE

• What distinguishes the Lordship of Christ from other people or powers who attempt to 'lord it over us' in today's world? (pp. 56–60)

• Name some ways in which 'our lives may be a prayer for the coming of [God's] Kingdom'. (pp. 60–61)

• What do the style, quality and purpose of our Church life proclaim about the Kingdom of God to those who do not yet recognise it? (pp. 63–64)

CHRISTIAN RESPONSE

• What sort of things have made the Church a curiosity or a threat (pp. 69–70) throughout the ages? What do we see as local, national or global signs of the influence of God's Kingdom (pp. 64–65, 68) and how do we reflect these in our Church life and mission?

• What might distinguish appropriate from inappropriate expressions of 'Kingdom values' in the tempestuous arenas of politics and social concern? (pp. 64–66) What would lend integrity to such Christian action and proclamation? (pp. 66–68)

• What sort of risky, prophetic gospel concerns and stances might the 'not yet' of God's Kingdom call us to as Christian people? (pp. 70–72)

ACTION

• Make a list of signs or possible signs and consequences of God's Kingdom for you and your church.

• Write these up on a large poster for display. Invite additions and comments.

• Produce prayers and meditations for home and congregational use from your shared work.

CLOSING PRAYER

Christlike God,
Transform us and all creation
by your suffering love and risen power.
For the sake of Jesus Christ, our servant-king. Amen.

# 4

# 'Come out from under your bucket!'

## Knowing, sharing and embodying the faith

'Sharing the faith' – that is our next theme. But by way of introduction, we will start several hundred years before Christ, in the middle of a war.

'What we are doing is not right.' The stark simplicity and bluntness of those words has never failed to impress me. They are the first words of four lepers who, in the interests of self-preservation, left the beseiged and starving city of Samaria and defected to their enemies and beseigers, the Syrians. Better to be a slave with food in your belly than to stand on your dignity and die of starvation!

But when they reached the enemy camp they found it deserted. So they not only stuffed themselves with food, they began plundering everything of value in sight, before they remembered the plight of their brothers and sisters. But when they did remember, they were overcome with remorse: 'What we are doing is not right. This is a day of good news and we are keeping it to ourselves.' (2 Kings 7:9)

Halted in their tracks by a sudden realisation of their wider responsibility, their story teaches us about finding the right perspective and following the right priority. In this

chapter I want to follow their example, regarding perspective and priority, in connection with sharing the faith. A
careful reading of the first chapter of St Paul's first letter
to the Thessalonians reveals a helpful pattern or formula.
I would sum it up thus: those who receive the faith must
share the faith and those who would share the faith must
first embody the faith.

That, basically, is the pattern I want to follow in this
chapter – knowing the faith, sharing the faith and embodying the faith.

## Soundbite and sound knowledge

We live in the age of the 'soundbite'. Media experts tell us
that people's concentration span is decreasing. If we have
something to say, which we want others to hear, it needs
to be said briefly and in a memorable manner. The most
popular news broadcasters, we are told, are those who are
masters of the memorable phrase. Indeed, many radio
reporters and television producers unashamedly inform
those they are interviewing that what they really want are
a few soundbites. Sustained argument, reasoned reflection
and sound knowledge all have their place but, when it
comes to communicating news in today's world, the soundbite, it seems, is the vital ingredient.

At this point I want to emphasise that I am not wishing
to disparage the concept of the soundbite. Indeed, a careful
study of the words of Jesus reveal his remarkable capacity
for producing them. Sayings like 'You must be born again',
'Give to Caesar the things that are Caesar's and to God the
things that are God's', 'What shall it profit a man if he gain
the whole world and lose his own soul', or even, 'Come
out from under your bucket!'[1] would have been meat and

drink to today's news journalists. Given the modern demand for instant, memorable and controversial comment, Jesus would have been a regular visitor to Broadcasting House and a prime target for the tabloid press!

But surely the reason why the memorable words of Jesus have moved the hearts and touched the deepest chords of human life in every age is that they sprang from an intimate knowledge of God. His words reflected the mind of God ('I speak just what the Father has taught me') and his life revealed the true image of God ('Anyone who has seen me has seen the Father').[2] Jesus sat under the word of God and absorbed it into his very being.

The best and most effective soundbites come from those who, like Jesus, have a sound knowledge and true grasp of their subject. This enables them to encapsulate profound truth in simple, if graphic, language. As Archbishop Robert Runcie once said, 'All intellectual illumination should mark progress towards greater simplicity.' If we are going to share the faith effectively the first prerequisite is for us to learn the faith. And that is a lifetime task. It is also a major task for the Church.

## Nurture is no optional extra

The One, Holy, Catholic and Apostolic Church is the means through which the purposes of God are made known. Its primary activities are the worship of God, the nurture of its members in discipleship, and mission in evangelism and service in the world. At the centre of those primary concerns is the nurture of its members. That nurture not only helps to form and inform their worship, it also serves to fashion and facilitate their mission in the world. Worship without nurture can be shallow. Mission without nurture can be superficial.

God's method of working in creation is full of interest and instruction in this regard. A careful study of the early chapters of Genesis indicate a pattern of growth from form to fullness. The creation of sea and sky, for instance, is followed by the creation of the creatures of water and air. In similar fashion the fertile earth is filled with creatures of the land. God's purpose for his children's growth and his Church's growth is no different. It is a pattern which moves from form to fullness. Like those newly born we are to desire pure milk, spiritual food, 'so that by it you may grow up'. We are called to 'grow up into Christ' who is our Head, 'to grow in the grace and knowledge of our Lord and Saviour Jesus Christ'.[3] Growth requires nurture. Nurture includes teaching. Teaching serves to increase our knowledge of the faith, especially when there is a practical application of that faith in our daily relationships and responsibilities.

Most people can understand the need for nurture and instruction for young or new Christians, in preparation for Baptism and Confirmation for instance. But there is still a great reluctance on the part of many to see themselves as disciples called and committed to a lifetime of learning, growth and development towards maturity in Christ. There are glorious exceptions, of course, but all too often the only conscious instruction in the faith that many receive is contained in the Sunday sermon. But how can such a limited diet, however palatable and creatively presented, possibly meet the needs of a congregation whose members are at various stages of their pilgrimage of faith? And how do preachers know that, under God, they are meeting the needs, stretching the minds, increasing the faith and changing the lives of their hearers, if there is no opportunity for come-back other than the doorstep comment 'lovely sermon, vicar'?

Surely the challenges facing the Church today require those who are not ordained, but who are so often at the frontiers of mission, to be ready and able to give a reason for the hope that is within them? Since, as we have already noted, 'the primary ministry of the great majority of Christians is their service of humanity in the everyday work of the world', is there not a need for Christians of all ages and in all walks of life to be regularly increasing their knowledge of the faith as it relates to their contemporary world?


NO LONGER CHILDREN

When the author of the letter to the Ephesians wrote to his readers, one of his central concerns was that they, as the Church in their locality, should become mature in their understanding and expression of the faith. They were not to be like children. He wasn't, of course, referring to those characteristics, like innocence and humility, which endear children to us and through which they become our teachers. Rather he was thinking of their ignorance and instability. He likens them to small boats at the mercy of storm-tossed seas, driven this way and that by unscrupulous people and unscriptural teachings.[4]

As a young curate I was given the gift of a bookcase – you know, the kind that swivels round on a central pedestal so that you can, with a gentle push, send it spinning and get to the many books which it holds so attractively. The gift became a thing of beauty and joy to me. To my children it became a source of wonder and delight. They spent hours spinning it round and I had to stand guard in case they hopped on to it and used it as a merry-go-round. They still refer to it as the 'whirligig'. It provides a classic picture of the kind of danger the writer to the Ephesians warns the Church against – a lack of maturity and stability that makes it easy prey to pressures which threaten to push it off course. There have been many times in recent days when the Church at both national and local level has revealed all the characteristics of the 'whirligig'.

By contrast, the author of Ephesians pleads for the Church to build itself up in love and to grow towards that stage of maturity that befits the Church as the place of Christ's presence and rule. He has a vision of the Church corporately mature in its grasp of the faith and its procla-mation of the truth. He has in mind the growth to maturity of the whole Church yet it clearly depends on the matur-ing of its individual members.

BUT . . . BE GROWN-UP

For such a vision to come to reality it requires the help of God's Holy Spirit for he is the supreme teacher. But we must not collude with the suggestion that we can leave the matter entirely to him. The realisation of the vision also demands a lot of hard work, imagination and personal commitment on the part of individual leaders and members of the Church, together with a corporate determination on the part of the whole. 'Work – for God is at work in you.' (Philippians 2:12)

The vision of a Church, and the individual members of it, becoming mature in knowledge of the faith must not be left in the realm of wishful thinking. The situation is too challenging and urgent for that. The multi-cultural mix of today's society, with the inroads of secularism increasingly persistent and the presence of other faiths a more dominant factor, demands that Christians, if they are to function as 'salt and light' in that society, must have a working

knowledge of the faith they professs. Proper strategies need
to be devised to turn the vision into a reality. Anglicans,
for instance, must confront and correct the perception that
many still have of Confirmation as the 'passing out parade'
of new disciples: the ceremony that marks their successful
completion of the only required period of instruction in the
faith. Other churches may have similar challenges to face.

Discipleship is a lifetime experience. So also is learning
the faith out of which that discipleship emerges. We must
take on board the concept of all-age learning, for while the
faith is that which 'has been once and for all entrusted to
God's holy people'[5] it is not prepackaged and labelled for
every eventuality. The faith is not a dead but a living thing.
It is not just something to be believed, as it were, and
tucked away in the bottom drawer either to preserve its
purity or to be kept for the proverbial rainy day. Rather it
is something in which we freely and creatively live. It has a
bearing on our age, our culture and every contemporary
situation.

I frequently hear lay people introduce their contribution
to a discussion or debate with words like, 'Of course I am
not a theologian'. And all too often, to their shame and my
embarrassment, I hear clergy say the same thing, suppos-
edly out of false modesty. The truth is that we, clergy and
laity, are all 'jobbing theologians'. We can't be otherwise if
we are to know and apply our faith to our life in the world.
Whether we like it or not we are in the business of applied
theology.

When I am ordaining or licensing clergy I am lawfully
required to remind them that the Church is called upon to
'proclaim the faith afresh in each generation'. It is a very
significant charge. It involves the whole Church, ordained
and non-ordained, the whole people or *laos* of God. All of
us are faced with issues in the world and in society today
which those early disciples could never have imagined, even

in their wildest dreams. Indeed, we are confronted with challenges, in the field of ethics and morality for instance, which our parents and grandparents never faced. That's why the faith needs to be proclaimed afresh to this and every generation. It is not a new faith but it is a new generation. And the old faith has got to be communicated in a manner which is pertinent to the present day. That demands hard work, serious thought and a willingness to learn.

## Help for the task

The community of the faith also requires imaginative strategies and realistic resources. The Church of England needs to take adult education more seriously. Prayer groups, house groups and study groups all have a place, as do good preaching and teaching. But there is need for a common policy right across the Church and a concerted effort in every diocese to implement it. Some local churches will have adequate resources in people and money to mount and maintain an effective adult education programme. Others will need the help of central resources. In this connection I believe that every diocese in the Church of England should have what might be called 'a foundation course' – an ongoing adult education programme in which people not only learn the faith but are also encouraged to reflect upon its bearing upon today's society and culture.

A course of this kind needs to be brought close to the local church and to be aware of its special needs. It needs to be flexible in its requirements and to provide opportunities for people to 'top up' their knowledge of the faith as occasion and the local situation demand. All too often such courses are used to prepare people for service in the

Church, as lay assistants of one kind or another. This is fine, as far as it goes, but I long to see courses used increasingly to equip ordinary Christian people for their life and service in the world.

Given that the demands upon ordinary Christian people can be very considerable, such training schemes must be creatively and attractively presented with the sensitive use of modern educational skills and technology. There really is no excuse for presenting the tenets of a life-changing faith in a dull and boring manner. It must also have a sense of reality about it. Thirteen weeks engaged in a detailed study of the Epistle to the Hebrews may be really gripping stuff, provided it meets people where they are and addresses the life questions which they face. If it fails to do that it could be a dreadful self-indulgence and a time-consuming irrelevancy. It must also recognise that different people learn in different ways. Not everyone is 'bookish'. Some like the 'lecture' style while others are put off by it. Some function better in groups, where there is animated discussion, while others prefer to listen in silence and reflect in private.

But in pleading for a realistic policy for adult education I am asking that such a policy be seen as part of an overall strategy for all-age learning in the Church. It ought not to begin in the Church. Ideally it begins in the home. But then, how many churches have a strategy for teaching new parents within their congregations how to teach their children the faith? I have a feeling that the demise of many Sunday schools has led to a dearth of an effective teaching of the faith to our younger children. If this is so, then every effort must be made to put it right. What is beyond question is that those who preach on Sunday must assume less and less regarding knowledge of the faith on the part of their hearers.

And learning ought not to end with the arrival of the bus

pass or the pension book. We tend to permit too much disparaging talk about ageing congregations as though at sixty plus people had passed their sell-by date as regards their contribution to the life and witness of the faith community. There is a third age of people in our communities for whom 'a refurbished theology of ageing will be required. Such a theology will move from viewing older adults as passive recipients of care. Ministry *to* older members will give way to ministry *by* older members.'[6]

At the beginning of life and towards the end of life, and at all ages and stages in between, we are called to grow as disciples of Jesus. The Church must help to encourage and facilitate that growth through an integrated programme of all-age learning. There is some superb resource material available, from agencies like the Church Pastoral Aid Society, for instance, to make this a practical possibility. And in every diocese and deanery in the country there is a resource in people and expertise to make it work – if only we have the will to turn the vision into reality.

One thing is clear: there never was an age in which the effective communication of the faith was more vital. It is crucial that members of the Church, the community of faith, in contributing to that task, are able to articulate the faith, according to the gifts God has given them, in a meaningful and winsome manner. It was Plato who said, 'Seven years are needful for a man to learn the truth, but fourteen in order to learn how to make it known to his fellow men.'[7] Plato's order of priority was right. We must know the faith before we can make it known. Whether we need a further fourteen years to learn the skill of communicating the faith is another matter. To that we must now turn.

## Come out from under your bucket

'What we are doing is not right. This is a day of good news and we are keeping it to ourselves.' The four lepers had made a life-saving discovery. Such good news, they were convinced, needed to be shared with their friends immediately. It would have been selfish in the extreme to have kept it to themselves.

In his Sermon on the Mount Jesus taught a similar truth when he referred, in a graphic and humorous fashion, to the folly of lighting a lamp and placing it under a bushel so that its light was hidden. In other words when you get something which by its very nature is meant to be shared it is both foolish and selfish to withhold it from others.

Behind this image of light, and undergirding this rather homely illustration, was an even more profound truth. In the Fourth Gospel we read that Jesus said, 'I am the light of the world'. That is, John's Gospel describes him as the light in which all else is illuminated and without which nothing ultimately makes sense.[8] But Jesus made an even more staggering claim when he said to his disciples in the Sermon on the Mount that they are the light of the world, the city set on a hill rather than being hidden in the valley, the lamp placed on a stand rather than hidden under a bucket or a meal tub.[9] The lesson is clear and unequivocal. The disciples of Jesus have the responsibility of being light-bearers and story-tellers. The light is for shining, not hiding. The story is for telling, not withholding. The world's true health and wholeness depend upon it.

It was the urgency of this fact that convinced the Lambeth Conference of Anglican Bishops in 1988 to pass the following Resolution: 'This Conference, recognising that evangelism is the primary task given to the Church, asks each Province and Diocese of the Anglican Communion, in co-operation with other Christians, to make the closing years of this millennium a "Decade of Evangelism" with a renewed and united emphasis on making Christ known to the people of his world.'[10] The Lambeth Bishops didn't, as it were, stumble on a new idea. They simply wanted to reinstate the priority of an old one, though, in doing so, they ran the risk of appearing to contain or imprison evangelism within a mere decade. It will have been a risk worth taking if during the Decade the Church can recapture the vision of evangelism, not as a periodic activity occasionally appearing on its agenda but as part of the regular heartbeat of its life.

NO ROOM FOR ELITISM

Technically, evangelism is the proclamation of a message. It is a telling forth or sharing of the good news of the victory of love as shown in the life, death and resurrection of Jesus. At its simplest, and perhaps most profound, it is the telling of a story of which we ourselves have become a part. Evangelism is not an activity to be set over against mission for it is an integral part of mission. Nor must we allow a wedge to be driven between evangelism and the work of the Kingdom, for the telling of the Jesus story becomes an invitation to those who hear it to share in the life of the Kingdom of God. Indeed, evangelism has been defined as 'that set of intentional activities which is governed by the goal of inviting people into the Kingdom of God for the first time'.[11] Kingdom theology and an enthusiasm for evangelism belong together.

Similarly, evangelism must not be seen as the exclusive preserve of a so-called spiritual elite. It is in one way or another the responsibility of every Christian and every congregation. The trouble is that evangelism has so often been caricatured in a way that puts it beyond the reach of most ordinary people in most ordinary congregations. The evangelist is often portrayed as an extrovert, deeply immersed in biblical knowledge, fearless in witness, and with the gift of the gab. Now it is true that some people are specifically called to be 'evangelists' in the technical sense of that word. They are endowed with the gifts of an evangelist and are trained and deployed to serve the Church in that particular capacity. But to suggest that they alone have the responsibility for sharing the good news would be foolish, for nothing could be further from the truth.

In the same way we must refuse to collude with the idea that the work of evangelism is restricted to the clergy. It is ordinary Christian people, so ideally placed in society, who must be at the forefront of any evangelism strategy the Church may have. The primary location of such people, being in society at large and only secondarily in the institutional church, makes their ministry of love, caring and witness vital to the task of evangelism. Wherever I go I meet ordinary Christians who are, unselfconsciously, day by day, telling the story of faith and commending Jesus. They do it by the quality of their lives, by their service to the community, by their courage and love in the face of adversity and by a thousand different ways.

THE IMPORTANCE OF PERSONAL RELATIONSHIPS

It is reckoned that over eighty per cent of those who become Christians do so through friendship with another Christian. Among other things Christianity is about a personal relationship with God, therefore a relationship with another Christian is the most natural context in which to meet God. My own experience, as an incumbent or minister of several parishes, is that churches grow through the fringe members becoming committed and bringing with them a new fringe of friends and neighbours. The tragic reverse side of that particular truth is that often the core membership is so taken up with maintenance that they have few relationships outside the church! The recently committed are the most fertile ground for evangelism through friendships.

It is those natural relationships that provide us with opportunities to tell our story of faith. When you think of it, no one else meets people in the same way, in the same situations, as you and I do. Each of us has unique opportunities and unique relationships. If we can discern the uniqueness of our own living and working situation and the relevance of the gospel to it, not only will our own lives be enriched but also our own witness will be all the more authentic. The kind of evangelism I have in mind is within reach of all of us – a friendly word at the right moment, a willingness to 'walk alongside' and not impose, a valuing of people for their own sake and not as potential converts. To my mind that is the foundation of all true evangelism. 'The first step towards a more credible evangelism is repentance for our confusing evangelism with propaganda.'[12] It is my conviction that integrity in personal relationships is the only basis for effective communication of the gospel.

A careful reading of the letter to the Ephesians seems to me to give substance to that conviction. Indeed it could be said that one of the purposes of the writer is the evangelisation of our network of relationships. He pleads for his readers to bring their network of relationships into line with the gospel. The gospel is brought to bear on the themes of truth, honesty and forgiveness; respect, love and service; marriage, home and church. According to the author it is through this evangelisation, or 'gospelisation' of our characters and the whole network of our relationships, that we stand against evil in the world and become what we are – the Church through which the gospel is made known in the whole universe.[13] Thus, in our evangelism we are evangelised.

## RIGHT WHERE THEY ARE

All around us, and within that network of relationships, there are people trying to make sense of their lives – lives which are fragmented and so often broken in a hundred different pieces. There are thousands of people seeking an inner peace and a sense of purpose; multitudes struggling to make their marriages work or their finances stretch; hundreds who stand by feeling helpless as those they love grow weaker in illness. There are families whose lives have been shattered and their hopes destroyed through unemployment. There are people shouldering enormous responsibilities in industry and commerce, in government and in local communities, struggling against impersonal forces, endeavouring to remain hopeful, wanting to do a good job. There are decision-makers upon whose word our environment is changed for better or worse, whose judgements determine the creation or distribution of wealth. There are varieties of cultures with riches to share and there are anxieties that traditional values and ways are changing, to say nothing of the whole sub-culture of fear and violence. It is in such social surroundings that we are called to let the light of Jesus shine and to tell the Jesus story and our part in it.

It is not an easy assignment. Some are overwhelmed by the magnitude of the task and lose heart. Others rejoice that they are called for such a time as this and use their natural friendships and their network of relationships as a means of non-threatening evangelism. I believe that the latter way is the way of Jesus and if we are prepared to follow it we can rely on the help of his Holy Spirit. Patiently, humbly and sensitively we must ask the Holy Spirit to help us discern what is the bad news amongst our friends and the networks of our relationships – isolation, meaninglessness, despair, loss of hope. Then, with the creative help of that same Holy Spirit, to hold up before them that facet of the diamond of the good news which, in our experience, shines on and begins to alleviate the bad news. In other words, we must meet people at the point of their felt need. It is a distorted view of evangelism that sees it in terms of dragging people into church. Evangelism consists of meeting people, truly meeting them, right where they are.

## THE SURROUNDING CULTURE

And, if I may say so, true love of neighbour demands that we not only meet them where they are but also that we try to understand 'where' they are and 'why' they are where they are. My pet aversion is the person who asks me a question and never listens to the answer. But even worse is the person who insists on doing me good, even if it kills me. Jesus was not like that. When everyone else assumed, because it was so obvious to them in their 'do-goodery', that Bartimaeus wanted his sight back, Jesus afforded him the dignity of asking him a question, 'What do you want me to do for you?' and listening to the answer.[14] Our Lord realised that to restore the sight of a blind beggar would completely change his life, so he gave him the responsibility of making a choice. Jesus enhances, and does not remove, our responsibilities. And if we are to engage in sensitive evangelism we must have the courtesy to examine the context in which that evangelism is to take place.

To put it another way, if our evangelism is to be effective, and if it is to have integrity, we must pay particular attention to the culture that surrounds us and affects those we are trying to evangelise. We must be prepared to ask ourselves some hard questions. Why, for instance, in spite of our modern methods, our energy, our expertise and commitment, do we still fail to communicate the good news successfully to the vast majority of the population? What is there in our culture that prevents it from becoming 'gospel friendly'?

It was Pope Paul VI who said, 'The split between Gospel and culture is without doubt the drama of our time ... therefore every effort must be made to ensure a full evangelisation of culture, or more correctly, of cultures. They have to be regenerated by an encounter with the Gospel, but this encounter will not take place if the Gospel is not proclaimed.'[15] The question that the Church faces is how we proclaim the gospel to the sort of culture in which we live; a culture which is said to be 'undergoing a profound change in which we seem to be moving from secularism to spirituality and from human rights to nationalism and fundamentalism'.[16] We are told that we live not so much in a secular age as in a religious 'pick-and-mix' age where people draw on any spiritual resources that they find helpful and the only spirituality which is not accepted is that of institutional Christianity.

Context and culture are major questions that must be addressed more fully elsewhere but, if we are to make headway in the work of evangelism, wisdom demands that we pay heed to them. Future circumstances will reveal that we cannot ignore them. The Church must come to terms with them. We must have the courage and develop the skills to confront and challenge the changing culture of our day with the truth of the gospel. We need to learn the language of our age; we must discover appropriate ways of service; we must 'walk alongside' and be patient. We must trust in the long-term purposes of a loving God. We must not lose heart, but rejoice in the fact that though we carry the treasure of the gospel in 'jars of clay' – that is, despite our human frailty and weakness (perhaps, because of our human frailty and weakness) – God is prepared to use us, and does use us, in sharing that treasure with others.[17]

● TOUCHING THE HEM

It is on this note of human weakness and feelings of personal inadequacy that I want to end my comments about sharing the faith. Some folk will always have anxieties lest their perceived lack of knowledge of the faith will disqualify them from ever making it known effectively to others. There will be others who will be equally concerned at their perceived lack of ability in articulating what they know. My heart goes out to such people and I feel embarrassed (and sometimes a little angry for them) when I hear insensitive preachers exhorting them towards a pattern of mission and evangelism that, far from encouraging their participation, only serves to increase their feeling of inadequacy and isolation.

To such people, and I would wish to include myself among them, I want to hold out a simple image of evangelism which is within their reach and ability. It is the image of the hem, and it is based on the incident in the gospels when a needy woman came behind our Lord in the anonymity of a crowd, touched the hem of his garment and was healed of her affliction. She looked for and found 'a touching place', and it marked the beginning of a new life.[18]

I have a vision of the local Christian family coming together for worship on a Sunday and then scattering throughout the community during the rest of the week where they form, as it were, the 'hem' of Christ's garment, bringing the love and compassion of Jesus within reach; within reach of those who are not yet ready to cross the threshold of the church, not yet ready for the commitment of faith we so often demand in our preaching and require in the words of our liturgy, but who feel their need of God and are longing, sometimes unconsciously longing, for 'a touching place' – a place of acceptance, help, healing and wholeness. Throughout my work as a Christian minister I have found in every church those who serve as 'touching places' within the local community. To suggest to them that they might become spearheads for local evangelism would scare them out of their wits. Yet, beyond any shadow of doubt, their humanity, their approachability, their love for people and their sheer ordinariness, all add up to a presence or 'touching place' where others can stretch out a tentative hand and, perhaps, begin to take the first few trembling steps on their journey of faith.

Far from evangelism being the preserve of the experts, it is a privilege and a responsibility within reach of every individual Christian and every local congregation no matter how ordinary they may consider themselves to be. Evangelism is as much about presence as it is about proclamation.

## Don't talk of love – show me

But some will want to argue that such a model of evangelism is a 'cop out' from what it is meant to be, namely, a clear, concise and verbal proclamation of the good news. Such people might be willing to acknowledge that my image or model of the hem is basically pre-evangelism, a preparation of the ground for the real thing. May I, therefore, recall my readers to the pattern that I outlined at the beginning of this chapter, based on that spelled out by the author of the first letter to the Thessalonians. Those who receive, and therefore come to know, the good news must share the good news, and those who would share the good news must first embody the good news. It is the embodying of the good news that I wish to emphasise at this point. In the opening chapter of that letter the writer tells us that the gospel 'came to them' and they 'received it', indeed they 'welcomed it'. And from them the message of the gospel 'rang out' to the surrounding regions, but not before they had become a 'model' or embodiment of the gospel that they wished to share.[19]

So such a method of evangelism is not only eminently sensible, it is also clearly biblical. And the principle of it is also contained in those words quoted earlier from our Lord's Sermon on the Mount: 'Let your light so shine before others that they see your good works and give glory to your Father in heaven' (Matthew 5:16). In other words, disciples of Jesus are meant to be visual aids as well as audio aids to the gospel. People are the words with which God tells his story, which is not at all surprising when we consider that he is a God who became visible above all in the person of Jesus of Nazareth. This means that what we are is just as important as what we say, usually more so.

Any good teacher will know that for a pupil simply to repeat what he or she has been taught does not guarantee an understanding or a knowledge of the subject. It may just prove that the pupil has a good memory. The only way of knowing that the truth has been heard and understood is when it is assimilated into life and practice, when actions speak louder and clearer than words. Eliza Doolittle had the right idea when she sang, 'Don't talk of love . . . show me'. Eliza obviously understood that there was such a thing as communication beyond language.[20] It is a lesson that, all too often, the Church is slow to learn and, frequently, tends to forget.

COMMUNICATION BEYOND LANGUAGE

We tend to talk too much. We find it hard to believe that truth can be communicated without us saying something, and sometimes we labour under the misapprehension that ten words are better than five! We would do well to read carefully Kahlil Gibran's poem 'Speak of Talking'. The words of this Lebanese poet never fail to challenge me:

> You talk when you cease to be at peace with
> your thoughts;
> And when you can no longer dwell in the solitude
> of your heart you live on your lips, and sound is a
> diversion and a pastime.
> And in much of your talking, thinking is half murdered.[21]

It is not just a matter of articulating the faith in such a way that the mind of the other person can grasp it. It has as much to do with conveying a conviction that we are on a journey of faith and attracting others, by what we are, to come and share that journey with us. Such a conviction is not easily, nor is it always, communicated by words. And in my own experience of conversion and spiritual awakening it was the impact of a faith attractively lived out by another, rather than the power of verbal persuasion, that proved to be so influential.

In this matter of communication beyond language one simple incident stands out in my memory. While working in an inner-city parish in Nottingham my wife and I, because of the exposed position of the vicarage, were fairly susceptible to a regular and rather large group of vagrants who called at our door. Some were belligerent, others were courteous; some smelled of alcohol and many needed a bath; nearly all asked for money but most settled for food. All were poor. The acquired wisdom was to keep such

people in the entrance porch and serve them sandwiches
and tea. For this purpose we kept a special plastic mug and
plate in the bottom of the kitchen cupboard.

Over the years we never had many complaints. But one
person, a fellow countryman of mine, was a thorough nuis-
ance. He would come at all hours of the day and night,
often quite frightening in appearance, and we felt anxious
lest he should come when our younger children were alone
in the house. On one particular occasion he came at three
o'clock in the morning. I was angry and I told him, in no
uncertain terms, not to come back. But he did – the very
next evening. We were in church at the time and when we
returned home there he was, sitting as large as life in the
drawing room in front of a roaring fire. My young teenage
son had answered his knock on the door and invited him
in. Not content with that, he had prepared a tray covered
with a white linen cloth and on it was one of our best
china cups and saucers together with a plate full of ham
sandwiches and some home-made cakes. My son was giving
his cup a refill just as we arrived.

We didn't know whether to laugh or cry. Eventually I
think we did both. When we had recovered from the initial
shock we roared with laughter. Then we were more deeply
moved at the attitude of our son. He had seen his mother
and father entertain friends in this way so it was quite
natural for him to do what he did. As Christians we had
no doubt whatsoever that this man was a person of unique
value in the sight of God. I preached that kind of message
every Sunday – and the plastic cup and saucer were kept
ready as evidence of my sincerity!

Our son didn't preach. He welcomed him in and affirmed
his value by treating him as one of the family. The linen
tray-cloth, the best china and the warm fire spoke volumes.
That's communication beyond language and it is at the
heart of all true evangelism. Wasn't it St Francis of Assisi

who emphasised the same truth when he urged: 'Preach the Gospel at all times; use words if you must.'

## THE CURIOSITY OF FAITH

But this communication beyond language is even more powerfully expressed through the local church. There is no more effective evangelistic witness than the life of the local community of faith when it becomes the embodiment of the gospel it proclaims, when it not only preaches good news but is itself good news within the local community. If within the local congregation there is openness and accept-ance, love and support, honesty and healing, reconciliation, justice and peace, then it has good news indeed to offer the local community.

But, perhaps, there's a prior stage to offering good news. Perhaps even the suggestion that we have good news to offer sounds a little arrogant to those outside the Church. Is there a better way? I believe there is. It is the way of curiosity. 'What does this mean?' was a question asked by those who witnessed the spirit-filled life and actions of the local church on the Day of Pentecost.[22] They were curious about what was happening amidst the community of faith. That, to my mind, is the better way, namely, to reveal a quality of life and love through the local expression of the Body of Christ so that others are drawn towards it. The local congregation must show something of that wonderful and mysterious love of God which is able to transform both individuals and communities.

We will all have our own suggestions as to what might constitute such an attractive local Christian community, and I have mine, based on experience as a parish minister and Diocesan Bishop. Worship is the primary ingredient. Whatever the tradition of the Church it must communicate a sense of God's presence. People need to be drawn into an experience of the transcendent, to stand in awe and wonder before a mystery which, as they may eventually discover, has both a name and a shape. Welcome is also a necessary quality in a growing church. The community of faith must be turned outwards. I have said elsewhere that, like the saloons in old westerns, my ideal church would have 'batwings' for doors. They would swing easily outwards and inwards, allowing ready access – 'in for worship and out for service'. That is one of the marks of a church in which the Holy Spirit is active. The presence of the spirit of renewal produces an outward-looking rather than an inward-looking church. The concept of Word must also be a vital part of such a church. By that I mean that it must listen to and take seriously the questions that people are asking and teach the faith relevantly. It needs to be a place where honest doubt can be expressed without people being dismissed as unsound. Work is my final ingredient for such a church. It may seem a strange thing to include but I consider it to be of great importance to those who are beginning the journey of faith. We must allow such people to find a place where they can make a contribution to the life of the church. A true community of faith will place the participatory ingredient high on its agenda.

All this will add up to a warm, outward-looking people who pray and who ponder their faith. These are the essential ingredients of what Archbishop Robert Runcie called 'Thoughtful Holiness';[23] the kind of holiness which is attractive and which arouses a proper and productive curiosity.

GOD'S WORK OF ART

This 'corporate curiosity' is nowhere better expressed than in the letter to the Ephesians. One of its major themes is the concept of the Church as the Body of Christ, the community in which Christ by his Spirit dwells and through which he reveals his word and his way to the world around. Among the many evocative and enriching images of this truth outlined by the writer none, to my mind, is more stimulating and encouraging than his description of the local Christian community as God's 'handiwork' or 'work of art'.[24]

Like me, most of my readers will be quick to admit that the Church doesn't always feel like it or look like it. Rather, like the reverse side of a beautiful tapestry, we are more conscious of the tangled mess, the multitude of loose ends and the unattractive confusion which lies behind the scenes. Thank God, he is aware of and is merciful towards our shortcomings and, through his patience and grace, is able to produce from the tangles and tensions the 'work of art' he wishes to present to the world. Nevertheless it is a staggering and humbling truth that the local community of faith, by what it is and by what it does, is meant to reflect the mind and heart of God.

When Pavlova the Russian dancer was asked on one occasion, 'Why do you dance?', she is reported to have replied, 'Do you think I would have danced if I could have said it?' There are some truths that cannot be communicated by mere words. They can only be expressed by the passion and commitment of a life. 'God did not become incarnate in a book but in a body', for in Christ 'the Word became flesh and dwelt among us'. Jesus Christ was what God wanted to say above all things to his world. So also, as God through his Spirit takes up residence and dwells in the midst of his people, flesh is put upon words and the faith is embodied in a community.

Those who receive the faith must share the faith and those who would share the faith must first embody the faith. Those are priorities not just for some in the Church for some of the time, but for all in the Church for all of the time.

## Study session

OPENING PRAYER

Give us courage, God of all hope,
To say and hear the words, speak the life
and live the truth that you give us
in Jesus Christ.

READINGS

1 Thessalonians 1:4–10; Matthew 5:13–16.

MEDITATIONS

'Those who receive the faith must share the faith and those who would share the faith must first embody the faith.' (p. 76)

'Faith ... is something in which we freely and creatively live. It has a bearing on our age, our culture and every contemporary situation.' (p. 81)

'The story is for telling, not withholding. The world's true health and wholeness depend upon it.' (p. 85)

'Evangelism is as much about presence as it is about proclamation.' (p. 93)

'There is no more effective witness than the life of the local community of faith when it ... not only preaches good news but is itself good news.' (p. 97)

'God did not become incarnate in a book but in a body.' (p. 99)

OUR EXPERIENCE

• 'Of course I'm not a theologian' (p. 81). Practically speaking, what has helped (or could help) you best in widening and deepening your understanding of the Christian faith? (pp. 82–84)

• What do you see as the essential difference between evangelism and propaganda? (pp. 86–88)

• Who needs the good news and why? (pp. 89–92). How can we create 'touching places' in church and community for such needs to be met? (pp. 92ff)

CHRISTIAN RESPONSE

• 'There is still a great reluctance on the part of many to see themselves as disciples called and committed to a lifetime of learning, growth and development towards maturity in Christ.' (p. 78) Is this true in your church? If not, what is best promoting this commitment and how can it be improved? If so, brainstorm the major reasons for this reluctance and share ideas for overcoming them.

• 'Over eighty per cent of those who become Christians do so through friendship with another Christian.' (p. 87) What natural and unique opportunities for Christian witness exist within the lives of your church members? What appropriate (and, perhaps, inappropriate) forms might that witness take? (pp. 88–91)

• Considering both the Thessalonians' pattern of receiving, embodying, sharing (pp. 93ff.) and the need for 'communication beyond words' (pp. 94ff.), discuss how your church might best contribute towards making faith understood, lived and known within the community in which it is set.

ACTION

• Working in pairs who know and trust each other sufficiently, share the story of how you came to faith, or what motivates your Christian convictions. Help each other to express your faith story in everyday, non-jargon words.

• Put a book at the back of your church inviting questions (and answers) about the faith. Think about questions or comments made by those you know and meet outside the church too. Use this to inform your decisions about reaching, teaching, Christian education and evangelism.

• Consider starting, developing or collaborating with others on a Christian foundation course or similar. Where would you find the support and resource?

CLOSING PRAYER

God of the incarnation
whose word became flesh in Christ,
Help us never to render that flesh as mere words,
but to proclaim it afresh through every breath of our
    lives. Amen.

# Through a Glass Darkly

## The pursuit of truth in the mission of God

Sometimes, in a moment of madness or desperation, I look back over old sermons that I have preached – and almost always get a shock. Occasionally the shock is a pleasant one, more in the nature of a surprise. I hadn't realised I was so erudite in those days! More often than not the shock is less pleasant, indeed it is frequently embarrassing. How could I have been so naive to write, teach and preach such things, and in such a manner? Of course I did it in good faith and in total sincerity, but some of the things I said and wrote in those early days of ministry turned out to be wrong. My understanding of the text and the truth it conveyed was limited. This resulted in a proclamation that was, at best, misleading or, at worst, untrue. I was convinced of the truth of what I was imparting, but subsequent study, knowledge and experience have caused me to review what I had written or spoken and to revise it in the light of greater understanding.

Most, if not all of my readers, will have had experiences of a similar nature. There is a period in life, usually when we are young, when we feel we know everything and there is little more to learn. The further we go in life, however, the more we become aware of just how little we know. The more our knowledge increases the more we realise that we

are still only on the outskirts. The further we journey with
God the more we are conscious of the fact that he is a God
of surprises who supplies us with new insights into old
truths and leads us into new paths of discovery, understanding and awareness.

But God is not only the God of surprises, he is also the
God of truth. Indeed, Jesus promised that through his Spirit
we would be led into all truth.[1] Our task, and the task of
every disciple of Jesus, is to follow where he leads, and in
doing so to pursue and embrace truth – for therein lies our
true freedom.[2]

This chapter concerns that search for truth. God's word
and will have been revealed to us in Jesus Christ, through
the scriptures, and in the historical experience of the
Church. To search for truth does not imply that we have not
discovered that life-transforming truth which we have found
in Jesus Christ – quite the reverse. He is not only the means
by which we come to know the Father; he is the 'light in
which we see the light' (Psalm 39:9) of truth in the world
around us. To search for truth is a humble acknowledgement that, whatever our current understanding and grasp
of truth, as it is in Christ, may be, we have not plumbed
its depths, reached its boundaries or exhausted its supply.
There's more. There will always be more. No matter how
far we may have journeyed on the pilgrimage of faith or
followed as disciples along the pathway of truth, our seeing
is still ony partial. As yet, we 'see through a glass darkly'
and must continue to follow the one 'in whose light we
shall see light' until we behold him 'face to face . . . and
know, even as we are known' (1 Corinthians 13:12).

But if, as emphasised in the last chapter, we are called
to share the faith, we must have confidence in the truth
and nature of that faith for today. Only then can we share
it with conviction. Only then can we engage with contemporary society, without arrogance and without fear. If, in

the pursuit of his mission in the modern world, God is going to require us to cross new frontiers with him, then we are likely to face new experiences and new challenges. In that process we shall also discover that we don't have all the answers. We must be prepared to grapple with new questions, discover new truths or, at least, new insights into old truths. An open mouth and a closed mind is a deadly combination. All of us are bored by those who if they are not talking are not listening. We are more likely to encourage others to join us on the journey of faith if we reveal that we are true disciples, still learning, still listening, still following, still pursuing 'more' truth, from the God of truth.

That, in essence, is the purpose of this chapter. We shall look at truth which is already 'given' to us; truth to which we must respond and by which we shall be judged. And, because God is alive and active in his world, we shall consider the need to explore the truth that emerges from that activity. As we engage in the mission of God we have truth to share and we have truth to learn. So let us begin with an ancient question.

### What is truth?

This was Pilate's question during the trial of Jesus. Was it an expression of worldly scepticism or philosophical pondering? We may never know. By turning on his heel without waiting for an answer, Pilate showed that he didn't believe that Jesus, or anyone else for that matter, could give one.[3]

Nevertheless, by asking the question, whatever lay behind it, Pilate was expressing a view sincerely held by many people today, who are unsure whether there is such a thing as truth. Until recently many people thought that science told us what was truth. Today, however, there is some disillusionment around even with regard to science. In many people's minds it seems to have let us down. The scourge of pollution, for instance, has undermined the trust that many have had in science. The fact that the positive and exciting advances in medical science have also produced hitherto unheard of problems in the realm of medical ethics has likewise caused a loss of confidence in many. Besides, most scientists today recognise that there is more to the world than science can explain.

However, for most people today 'truth' is considered to be relative. 'Truth' means 'what is true for me'. I had a touching and somewhat amusing illustration of this from a five-year-old while I lived and worked in Yorkshire. She was the granddaughter of a sheep farmer and had been given a children's Bible book for Christmas. Soon after Christmas she came to her grandmother, a local church-warden, and holding out the book said, 'This Bible isn't true'. To say that her grandmother was surprised would be the understatement of the year. She was, as they say in that part of the world, 'gob-smacked'. But all became clear when the little girl turned the pages of the book to the pictorial story of Noah's Ark. Sure enough, as her small granddaughter pointed out, 'There's no sheep there, granny'. Every day this little girl was surrounded by sheep, they dominated her life. She couldn't imagine life without them. A story which told of all the animals of the world going into the Ark, accompanied by a picture that revealed that there was not one (let alone two) sheep among them, simply wasn't true to life. For the little girl, 'truth' was relative.

But, despite the attractiveness and apparent reasonableness of such a view, when it comes to the serious business of life it ultimately proves unsatisfactory, because it doesn't really work. This chapter is being written just at the

moment when thousands of people are gathering at Auschwitz for the fiftieth anniversary of its liberation by the Russian Army in 1945. We have all been movingly reminded
of the horrors perpetrated in that infamous place. Along
with most other people throughout the world we would
want to say that Auschwitz was objectively evil, not just
that I think it was evil and you are free to disagree. There
is something that is true about that world which stands
beyond all personal preferences and tastes. Tolerance is
a great virtue, vital to the health and wholeness of any
community. But it is a misuse of tolerance to press it into
service in such a way as to insist that any claim to objective
truth must be arrogant. That is unfair and untrue. Some
people are very intolerant in their insistence on making
'tolerance' into an absolute truth.

## The truth shall make you free

The New Testament says a great deal about 'truth'. This
is especially so in St John's Gospel where 'truth' is one of
its central themes. Indeed, as we have noted above, it is in
that Gospel that Jesus makes the claim that 'The truth shall
make you free': that is, free to be what we are meant to be,
sons and daughters of God rather than slaves to self and
sin. In this connection it is helpful to reflect on the parable
in St Luke's Gospel of the Prodigal Son, which is really a
story about a loving father. Though I have heard many
interpretations and read many commentaries on the parable, none has described the prodigal as arrogant for returning home from the far country (though some have described
him as arrogant for leaving home in the first place!). Yet it
was the objective truth of the nature of his father's home
and his father's love that eventually drew him from the life

of a slave to the freedom of a son. The truth which the parable declares about the father is really a reflection of the truth about God.[4]

Truth in the Bible is usually closely related to the nature of God. God is truth. 'Truth', therefore, is an appropriate concept for the historical, scientific, moral and spiritual realities of God's world; but ultimately truth is personal, 'I am truth', said Jesus.[5] He is the truth that makes us free. In other words, the New Testament works with the concept of revelation; that God makes known true things about himself and his world, especially through the Word, Jesus Christ, who is God's personal truth embodied. John expressed the conviction of those early disciples, who were in no doubt that there was something objectively given: 'We proclaim to you what we have seen and heard.' His phraseology is graphic: 'we have *heard*, we have *seen* with our eyes, our hands have *touched*'. That is, 'the Word became flesh and thus presented himself to our three higher senses (hearing, sight and touch). To have heard was not enough; men *heard* God's voice in the Old Testament. To have *seen* was more compelling. But to have *handled* or touched was the conclusive proof of material reality, that the Word was "made flesh and dwelt among us".'[6]

Christianity has developed an entire theology on the premise that Jesus of Nazareth, the Messiah, was crucified, died, was buried, and was raised to life again. But it has done so on the basis of what God has revealed. So, far from appearing arrogant in claiming to believe in objective truth, it would seem more arrogant to refuse to believe in that which God has claimed to reveal to us in his Son Jesus Christ.

## Stagnant pool or flowing stream?

But as well as its emphasis on revealed or objective truth the New Testament also has a strong emphasis on 'searching'. It is unwise to claim, as someone did in my hearing quite recently, that 'we "have" the truth, and that's the end of the matter'. Such an attitude is hard to justify from the scriptures. It is not that we 'have' the truth all sewn up, as it were, but through the Spirit we are being drawn towards the truth as it is in Jesus.

Jesus was the wisest of teachers. He didn't try to teach truth before his disciples were ready to receive it. 'I have much more to say to you, more than you can now bear', he said to them, 'but when he, the Spirit of truth, comes, he will guide you into all truth' (John 16:12–13). In other words, when they were ready to receive it they would be led into a deeper and richer understanding of the truth in Jesus Christ. We must resist the temptation to turn God's truth in Christ into 'a stagnant pool instead of a flowing stream'.[7] That would make a travesty of the ministry of the Spirit as promised by Jesus.

The theme of searching and seeking is not restricted to isolated texts or incidents. Great sections of the gospel records are given over to it. Much of St Luke's Gospel is about journeys, during which the truth is disclosed by words and deeds. As the disciples accompanied Jesus on his journeys throughout Galilee and towards Jersusalem they turned out to be journeys of discovery. By what he said and did they came to know truth about prayer, discipleship and forgiveness, about wealth, joy and the Passion. Their progress was not measured so much in miles travelled as in truth discovered.

The classic story of a journey turning out to be a pilgrimage towards truth is that which took place on the road to Emmaus after the Resurrection. It was not just a journey through the lonely roads outside Jerusalem, it was also a journey through the scriptures with Jesus as the commentator. The two dispirited disciples are taken gently but firmly from the darkness of their disappointment and self-pity into the increasing light of the truth of the Resurrection. Their hearts are warmed in the process and finally their eyes are opened and they see the stranger who had walked with them on the road as their crucified and now risen Lord. Their progress towards Emmaus was a progress towards truth.[8]

Progress towards truth was also the theme of so many of the metaphors used by St Paul. He speaks of 'running the race and fighting the fight'. He longs for likeness to Christ but his integrity compels him to admit that he is not there yet, 'not that I have already obtained all this, or have already been made perfect, but I press on to take hold of that for which Christ Jesus took hold of me . . . I press on towards the goal to win the prize' (Philippians 3:12, 14). Paul knew that being made in the divine image was both a gift and a task: to become what we are – to grow into the measure of the stature of the fullness of Christ, that is into authentic humanity.

## An important balance

So there is a balance in the New Testament between truth revealed and truth discovered; between receiving truth and searching for truth. The Christian faith is rooted in history. It is a story in which God acted through particular people and particular events and, supremely, through Jesus Christ our Lord who, 'was declared to be the Son of God, by his resurrection from the dead' (Romans 1:4). But though rooted in history it is not imprisoned in history. The story goes on and the journey continues. It is a living faith, centred upon one who is not only the Lord of history but also the Lord of the present and the future. We must therefore pursue and expect new things from the God of newness and truth.

This balance between revealed truth and searching for truth is of vital importance for the Church in mission. Why?

## TRUTH TO TELL

First, it is because there is something to share. It is possible for people to have true knowledge of God. Such knowledge will not be exhaustive but it can be none the less true and trustworthy. In the last analysis witnesses are required to give testimony not to conjecture or hearsay but to what they believe to be true.

It would be difficult to read the New Testament and not come to the conclusion that the Church proclaimed the good news with conviction because it believed it to be true and was prepared to suffer for it. No amount of wishful thinking on the part of those early disciples could have produced the courage and determination they showed in sharing the faith. The pressures they came under to deny it were intense and life-threatening. But the truth that they discovered in Jesus was life-transforming. What they had seen and heard and experienced combined to convince them that what they shared was not fantasy but truth.

While there is never any excuse for arrogance in sharing the faith, there is no need for apology. We are not proclaiming good ideas. We are not purveyors of good advice. We are sharing good news based on truth revealed to us by God through Jesus Christ.

According to the second letter to Timothy, the experienced Paul instructs young Timothy in such matters: he reminds him and us that we are commissioned to 'guard the truth'. He speaks of it as a precious treasure entrusted to his charge. It is not to be eroded by neglect but preserved with care. It is a treasure deposited for safe-keeping with the Church. Christ had entrusted it to Paul who now entrusts it to Timothy.[9]

But, of course, it is a trust laid upon the Church in every age. Those who are teachers in the Church are required to 'rightly handle the word of truth'. That is, those who are called to communicate the faith to others are to 'make it a straight path' (rightly handle). There is to be an accuracy and an aptness in the way we share the faith so that it is made easier for others to follow. We are so to preach and teach that we enable people to listen to the truth.[10]

The common testimony of the Church in every place and in every age is that it has been put in trust with the gospel – and that gospel is true. There is no room for complacency but every reason for confidence in the good news we share.

PARTNERS TOGETHER

Secondly, this balance is important for mission because, in the human family we are all partners together in the search for a clearer understanding of God. I find this particular thought both encouraging and exciting in terms of mission. It is not a subtle way of saying that 'all roads lead to God', for that is a concept which I find difficult to accept. But it is a recognition that all men and women are made in the image of God and, therefore, it is not at all surprising that deep in the hearts of all people, at least at some stage of their lives, there will be a desire, a longing, a search for a clearer vision of the divine. It was surely this truth that was at the back of those famous words of St Augustine, 'Our hearts are restless until they find their rest in Thee'.

However, it is not just the unconscious search of those who claim no religious allegiance or affiliation that I find exciting when considering the mission of the Church. It is the search that goes on continually within the Church itself. It is a co-operative activity. The author of Ephesians places emphasis upon this corporate search when he reminds us that it is 'with all the saints' (Ephesians 3:18) that we may have the power to comprehend the love of God.

Nearly forty years ago my wife and I visited the Glens of Antrim, a well-known beauty spot in Northern Ireland, for the first time. We were held spellbound by a waterfall with its silver cascade standing out in sharp and beautiful contrast to the dark grey rocks and the dark green foliage. It was an amazing sight. But when we moved into a little log cabin further up the valley and discovered a multi-coloured viewing window, suddenly, as we looked through it, the silver cascade became a kaleidoscope of colour and beauty. It was truly breath-taking. The rich diversity and combination of colours served only to enhance and add splendour to that which was already beautiful.

I find that experience remarkably helpful in understanding those words from Ephesians. God has made each of us unique. He has equipped each of us with distinctive gifts and personalities, but so that we can make our special contribution to the beauty of the whole picture. As the creative light of God's Spirit is allowed to shine through those gifts and personalities, so the multi-splendoured love of God is seen in all its glory. There is a very real sense in which the whole love of God can only be perceived in the whole people of God.

Such a truth is crucial to the mission of the Church. It means that no one is without significance. We need each other. We are accountable to each other. We learn from one another. The scholar and the mystic, the introvert and the extrovert, the dreamer and the activist, all have a part to play, and all have played their part throughout the ages. Our search for God and for growth in his truth and love need not take us into some rarified spiritual atmosphere accessible only to the elite. Rather it will draw us closer to one another in the hurly-burly of everyday life, so that, 'we may have power, "together with all the saints", to grasp how wide and long and high and deep is the love of Christ'.

Given this vision of co-operative activity of search and growth in the truth and love of God, surely the Church must take some urgent and practical action to foster, enable and resource such activity? At both local and national level we need to develop educational programmes to help one another be better disciples (learners). I have already touched upon this in the previous chapter but the point cannot be stressed too often and we ought not to stop calling for it until it becomes a practical reality.

Another way of explaining or expounding those words from Ephesians was supplied by a child writing in his school work-book. He wrote, 'People are the words with which God tells his story'. As is so often the case with children, he got to the very heart of the matter with directness and simplicity. If indeed God does tell his story through people, and a study of the scriptures and the history of the Church seems to confirm that, then one of the most important things we can do is to help one another become better 'story-tellers': that is, better expressions of God's love, truth and grace; in other words, better disciples.

## Dialogue between disciplines

When I became a new Christian in my late teens I immediately came under pressure to obey a call, expressed in words of scripture taken out of context, to 'Come out from among them and be separate'. It was an emotional appeal, on the part of some of my friends, to leave my spiritual home in the Church of Ireland and take up residence in a 'purer' church environment free from doctrinal pollution. It was also a plea for me to keep myself from contamination by reading only the 'right' books, keeping company only with the 'right' people and having nothing whatever to do with those so-called 'destroyers of faith', namely, scientists and historians. And all this to ensure that I remained in the 'truth'.

Thank God for equipping me with a rebellious temperament! Even in those early days I saw through the shallowness and folly of such teaching. Common sense told me that there were not two kinds of truth – God's and some other kind. All truth is God's truth. There is no other kind of truth.

That fact liberated me from the fear of moving away from so-called safe places and people. Though I am an extremely poor sailor, it gave me courage to move out from the shallows into uncharted waters. It encouraged me to see the importance of dialogue between the disciplines. Despite what my self-appointed spiritual 'minders' told me, there is no divide between science and faith or between history and faith. Clearly there are points of disagreement but increasingly there appear to be convergences in many areas of common concern. Many scientists who are Christians, for instance, look upon their work as contributing to our knowledge of God's world and, therefore, conducive to a deeper wonder as we reflect upon his wisdom and power. There are many scientists who believe that modern science, objectively understood, is not in conflict with, but rather supports and underpins our faith. While it may be an over-statement to describe theology and science as 'willing and compatible bed-partners',[11] it would be wide off the mark to see them as 'unequally-matched sparring partners'. 'There may be aspects of truth to which religion is the gate, as indeed there are aspects of truth to which particular sciences are the gate. But if there be a creator, and if truth be one of his attributes, then everything that is true can claim his authorship, and every search for truth can claim his authority.'[12] That is as true in the realm of history as it is in the realm of science.

Since all truth is God's truth, Christians above all people need have no fear of truth wherever it is found. As we pursue the mission of God we will need to open ourselves to search for truth in dialogue with disciplines of many kinds, and with groups either hostile to or ignorant of the faith. Such programmes of creative encounter could be established, in Anglican terms, at parish, deanery or diocesan level. It will be a painful process but one eminently worthwhile, if truth is the goal.

## Dialogue between faiths

If dialogue between disciplines is important, so also is dialogue between faiths. Indeed, for the health and well-being of a society which is becoming increasingly multi-faith, it is crucial. Professor Hans Kung put the issue in stark but realistic terms when he said, 'No survival without a world ethic. No world peace without peace between the religions. No peace between the religions without dialogue between the religions'.[13]

For most of us, however, our interest or involvement in

inter-faith dialogue will not be determined by such stark realities. The conviction that gradually dawned upon me during my time as Bishop of Bradford was that the only future we had in that community was a future together: a future in which bridges were built across the faiths rather than barriers erected between them; bridges built on the foundations of mutual respect, understanding and tolerance, and extended and strengthened by dialogue and service to the community.

But dialogue should not just be for the purpose of building good community relations, important as these are. In our search for truth we can learn from one another something of the ways of God. Some people feel that to engage too closely with those of other faiths is to do despite to our own convictions. But that is not so. On the contrary, convictions rather than indifference are the better guarantees of tolerance. As the late Archbishop Lord Ramsey said, 'People steeped in the laziness of mutual and moral indifference are apt to pride themselves on being tolerant; they are not. There is none of the nobility of those who, with strong and passionate convictions, yet discipline themselves painfully not to trample on the convictions of others. True tolerance implies convictions. The tolerant man, however, reverences the processes by which he reached his own convictions – the processes of reason, argument, intuition and conscience – and he therefore reverences the same processes at work in another man which leads that man to his own convictions.'[14]

To put it another way, those Christians who break free from the fear and complacency that so often inhibit them and enter into constructive and creative dialogue with those of other faiths, can experience a marvellous enrichment and a fresh understanding of their own faith as well as making progress in the common search for truth.

It needs to be clearly understood, however, that the way

of dialogue is not a soft option. Dialogue involves risk and it entails vulnerability. Some would want to draw too sharp a distinction between mission and dialogue. But they are not mutually exclusive, nor do they have to be seen as stark alternatives. If the call to mission requires that I take my faith seriously then, if I am to follow the example of the one on whom my faith is focused, I will take seriously the faith of the one encountered in dialogue, together with the spiritual insights of the tradition from which that person comes. If, as I believe, mission involves searching for truth, then dialogue with others is both a privilege and a responsibility. Mission and dialogue can promote a better understanding of faith, of one another, and of God.

## A larger vision

One of the things that militates against constructive dialogue between people of different faiths is an insensitive triumphalism on the part of some Christians. The words 'Jesus is Lord' formed the primitive creed of Christianity, and the core of the Christian faith. This confession has also been a key element in Christian proclamation in every age. There is no way that Christians, with integrity, can soft-pedal or downplay such a confession; to do so would be a denial of our faith.

Sometimes, however, it is proclaimed in such a manner as to imply that every other faith, therefore, is 'rubbished' as a result. Of course, that is not the intention behind the proclamation but, often, that is the way it is heard in other faith communities. It is my conviction that a loss of triumphalism can lead to a greater understanding and acceptance as long as it is replaced by a larger theology of the *Logos*; a sensitive and biblical proclamation of the cosmic Christ.

John, in his gospel prologue, and Paul, in his letter to the Colossians, spell out this larger vision. 'In the beginning was the Word, and the Word was with God and the Word was God.' The writer is saying that Jesus Christ is the Word, that is, the one who stands before all time and space, the author of the creation of which he has become a part. He is the perfect expression of all that God is and thinks and desires for men and women. 'God is Christ like, and in him is no unChrist-likeness at all'.[15] Paul reinforces such an understanding when he declares that the very nature and character of God has been perfectly revealed in Christ; and that in him the invisible has become visible. But not only is he Lord of the Church, writes Paul, he is also Lord of the cosmos. Even cosmic principalities and powers, from the highest to the lowest, are subject to him. Christ is unique, for he is the ultimate goal of all creation and in him all things hold together and without his sustaining power they would disintegrate.[16]

The point I wish to make, in the light of these things, is that if all this is embodied in Jesus – if he indeed is the creator, sustainer and goal of all that is – can he not also be heard outside the Christian Church? Given that he 'fills all things', can we genuinely believe that he is totally absent from other faiths? What has God been doing all these years? This is not to say, I repeat, that all roads lead to God and that all religions are the same (my Muslim, Sikh and Hindu friends would not agree with such superficial comments), but it is a conviction that the Spirit of God is at work beyond the Church. And if he is at work in the secular world it would seem strange if he were not at work among those who are sincere seekers after God. It is for that reason that I believe the Lordship and uniqueness of Christ, in which I firmly believe, must be presented with sensitivity, courtesy and understanding.

## Heart of the matter

Nevertheless, although our proclamation of what we believe to be true needs to be sensitive, we must hold firmly to the central truths of the faith. Our friends in other faiths would expect no less and their respect for us would diminish if we failed to do so.

Basic to those beliefs is the Incarnation: the belief that in Jesus God came personally among us. And in that coming he was embodied in a human life. He involved himself patiently, unconditionally and sufferingly in the details of that human life. It was Jesus himself who said, 'He who has seen me has seen the Father'; in other words God as Father is revealed in and by Jesus.[17] In Jesus, God becomes visible and tangible. He is revealed not as a remote and distant ruler who stands aloof from his creatures but as one who takes the initiative and, without preconditions, comes alongside his children, all his children, in passionate concern for them. The incarnation is God's 'yes' to humanity and, indeed, to the whole of creation. God does not have 'no go' areas. There is no part of his creation outside his loving interest and involvement. The incarnation speaks of a God who puts love for others before love for himself. It is probably best summed up in the words of St Paul: 'Have this mind among yourselves, which is yours in Christ Jesus, who, though he was in the form of God, did not count equality with God a thing to be grasped, but emptied himself, taking the form of a servant, being born in the likeness of men. And being found in human form he humbled himself and became obedient unto death, even death on a cross.' (Philippians 2:5–8)

A God who willingly exchanges richness for humility is a mystery we cannot hope to fathom. A God who lays aside power and enters into weakness is foreign to our idea of sovereignty. Nevertheless, it seems that weakness is the glory of God. If we want to see the glory of the God of Incarnation we must look not to a throne but to a smelly stable and a blood-stained cross. Perhaps it is in this voluntary vulnerability that the uniqueness of Christ and Christianity is to be found. And that brings us to another core truth to which we must hold firmly in all our teaching and in all our searching.

## Cross and Resurrection

The New Testament not only reveals that God came personally among us in the Incarnation, it also declares that in the Cross and the Resurrection the specific purpose of his coming is spelled out. The divine instruction to Joseph in preparation for our Lord's birth was, 'You are to give him the name Jesus, because he will save his people from their sins.' (Matthew 1:21) The rest of the New Testament is consistent in its teaching that such a saving purpose would be achieved through the Cross and the Resurrection. However, we must be careful not to drive a wedge between our Lord's life and his death. The self-emptying that culminated in his death actually began at his birth and, indeed, his identification with the lowly and the outcast, together with his casting aside of some of the current conventions of his day, brought about his crucifixion.

Nevertheless, 'The cross of Jesus is, uniquely, the badge of distinction of the Christian faith'.[18] When the risen Christ said to his disciples, 'As the Father has sent me so send I you', he immediately showed them his hands and his side. In other words when he commissioned his disciples to go on the same mission that he had received from the Father, it was the scars of the cross and passion that revealed who he was.[19] But the wounds of crucifixion did more than that. They created a pattern for all who wish to engage in mission to follow, namely, the way of self-empty-ing, suffering and service. There is no triumphalism here. The powerful and the self-confident are likely to accomplish less in the realm of mission than the weak and the poor.

The Cross, however, was not just a pattern for us to follow. Coupled with the Resurrection it is the means of our salvation. It is God's appointed way of redeeming the whole of humanity. Peter, for whom the Cross at one stage was abhorrent and from which he fled in fear, later came to see its full significance when he wrote, 'Christ died for sins once for all, the righteous for the unrighteous, to bring you to God' (1 Peter 3:18). Paul also emphasised this work of reconciliation when he wrote that 'God was reconciling the world to himself in Christ' (2 Corinthians 5:19) – an interesting insight from one who called the Cross foolish-ness and who reacted with persecuting zeal when he heard it preached.

Peter and Paul were writing in the light of the Resurrec-tion. It was the Resurrection that changed their view not only of the Cross but also of Jesus and of God himself. They saw the Resurrection as of fundamental significance to the Christian faith. Indeed, it is not too strong to say that they came to believe that the Christian faith stands or falls with the Resurrection; so much so that if there was no Resurrection there was no gospel to preach and no faith to hold.[20]

But we must not present the Resurrection in such a triumphalist way as to diminish the reality and significance of the suffering of the Cross. We must not proclaim the victory as though that was all that mattered. God's order is important. 'The order of the gospel story is irreversible and its contents cumulative.'[21] Resurrection is only reached through the Cross. The message of Cross and Resurrection is that Jesus died for us, all of us, and now lives for us, all of us. What God has joined together we must not put asunder. It is through Cross and Resurrection that humanity, all of humanity, is redeemed. In that sense 'there is no other name' in which humanity can be saved. It was at the Resurrection that 'God bestowed on Jesus the name that is above every name, that at the name of Jesus every knee should bow and every tongue confess, "Jesus Christ is Lord" to the glory of God the Father' (Philippians 2:9–11).

Holding firm to the revealed truth of the Incarnation, Cross and Resurrection, and their universal and cosmic significance, far from excluding those of other faiths, leads me to the conviction that in my search for truth I will find the grace of God at work among those who have not heard the name of Jesus. That is an incentive rather than a deterrent to mission.

## Grace and space

That the grace of God may be found at work outside the Church may surprise some; that it should be found at work inside the Church should not be totally unexpected! Though, to be frank, there is one particular grace which, in some churches, is frequently in short supply. I refer to the grace of encouragement. Church congregations need to cultivate a ministry of encouragement among their own members. Among the list of the gifts of the Spirit outlined by St Paul was the gift of encouragement.[22] It may not be considered one of the more important gifts, but in my humble opinion it is vastly underrated.

In every congregation there are those who need help in their search for greater knowledge of the faith and confidence in mission. Such help is usually more effective when it comes from another member of the congregation who has passed that way before and is aware of the kind of encouragement that ordinary people need and may be too hesitant or shy to ask for. I thank God for those ordinary, unsung people who went out of their way to encourage me to grow in the faith. Only now, as I look back, can I appreciate their unselfishness, patience and sheer good will. Every congregation needs people like that. They may not be high-profile leaders in the Church but they have been equipped with a very special gift.

One of my favourite New Testament characters has always been Ananias. He is little known and is only mentioned in the shadow of St Paul.[23] Yet it was Ananias who was responsible for encouraging Paul to become the great leader in the mission of God in those early days of Christianity. Paul was in Damascus following his miraculous encounter with the risen Jesus. He was blind, fearful and uncertain about the future. Ananias had the grace of encouragement, so God sent him to Paul. He was the ideal helper. He dealt with Paul in love and compassion, as a brother, and Paul was restored, strengthened and envisioned for the future. Ananias gave Paul encouragement in the faith and confidence in mission. Every church needs at least one Ananias and also a 'Barnabas', which means 'son of encouragement'.[24]

But if churches need to exercise the grace of encouragement they also need to provide space for people to explore doubts, confusions, difficulties and questions. Sadly, many churches do not have such a 'space'. They deal in certainties. There is no room for exploration. To question the faith is perceived as disruptive, to express open doubt is considered destructive. So people either tend to suffer in silence or, if they find that the Church is not a safe place to search for truth in that way, they gently fade away.

But if the Church is serious about effective mission it must be prepared to be exposed to questions people ask.

It must be seen as a safe place where honest doubts can be expressed and where confusions about the faith can be addressed. The level of faith commitment contained in our liturgy, for instance, is remarkably high, and the promises we make during much of our hymn-singing would, on the surface, indicate that we are in the premier league of Christian discipleship. Yet we all know that the reality can be quite different. Many of us struggle with the faith and with the Church. We live with the contradiction of the public face and the private person and the gap which so often exists between the two. If only more churches would acknowledge the gap and allow people to explore it in an honest, open and unthreatening manner, it would lead to maturity in faith and confidence in mission.

## The search goes on

Maturity in faith and confidence in mission is a vital combination if we are to face up to being effective Christian disciples in the third millennium. Being the Church in the world demands that we relate our faith to the challenges of an increasingly complex society. We can't go it alone. We need to help each other work at the implications of our knowledge of God's truth for our daily work and witness at business and at home.

While reflecting upon the content of this chapter I was involved in a two-day mission event in an urban area of the Southwark Diocese. During one of the evening gatherings two people were interviewed about their work and the relevance of their faith in relation to it. One was a social worker and the other the General Secretary of a trade union. I was riveted and inspired by the interviews. Here were two people committed to the mission of God, being put under the spotlight of a public interview before two hundred people and being ready and able to give a reason for the hope that lay within them. There were no pat answers, no clichés, only a genuine wrestling with the implications of their knowledge of the truth on the complexities of their working life and the demands of their homes and families. It was a moving experience for those who were privileged to be spectators – though actually, as we watched and listened, we ceased to be spectators and became fellow participants with them in their search to relate their faith to contemporary life and work.

Because we live in a rapidly changing world we are being faced with new situations which present us with challenges that we haven't encountered before and for which there are no pre-packaged answers. The road before us, as it were, is an unmarked one, with no signposts and the distinct possibility of taking a wrong turning and coming to a dead end. No one may have travelled this way before us. That makes us pioneers or trail-blazers with the responsibility to search and discover the path of progress, the right way ahead.

This is not a task for faint hearts, nor, perhaps, for those who are not prepared to live with uncertainties, contradictions and, sometimes, unresolved conflicts. But it is consistent with the Kingdom of God and the mission of God that we search for the truth of God that will enlighten the way ahead and help us all towards a right way of living in our contemporary society. We are not only to discover and believe truth, we are to live our lives according to it. The way we 'do the truth' in relation to the challenges of modern society is part of our mission. The writer of the letter to the Galatians seemed to have such a thing in mind when he wrote about 'faith expressing itself in love' (Galatians 5:6). Truth, like faith, is not meant to be a dead thing. The reality of it is to be seen in life and action.

That search, which needs to be ongoing, will take us into areas of concern at the individual, local and national level. The issue of personal and social ethics, for instance, is rightly very much on our national agenda. Increasingly difficult ethical issues are crowding the agenda of our daily living. They come at us in the home, in commerce and industry, in the realm of education and science, and in the world of politics. What are the implications of our knowledge of God's truth for such matters? There's still a lot of searching to be done. Satisfactory ways forward are often more difficult to discover than some people imagine.

The same is true in terms of 'Christianising' our society and its institutions. How can we bring Kingdom standards and values to bear upon the systems and the power structures that are so determinative of our daily lives? How can we help to influence the establishing of Christian patterns of work? How can we engage meaningfully with our changing culture? And, crucial to all this, how can we address these matters and communicate in a language that others can understand and to which they can respond? In these and in many other areas of challenge and opportunity we must continue the search for truth.

This chapter began with a personal admission: some of my old sermons, in the light of knowledge and experience, had to be revised. It ends with a personal conviction: God has revealed himself in scripture, in history and, supremely, in Jesus Christ. But that is not the end of the matter; in many ways it is the beginning. Since it is in his light that we see light, the more we come to know God in Christ the greater will be the light and truth that we receive. But that is the work of a lifetime. Becoming a disciple of Jesus involves us not only in mission but also in a lifetime of following, learning and searching. If we stop searching we will stop learning. If we stop learning then, to all intents and purposes, we will have stopped following. If we stop following, then we will have forfeited our share in the mission of God.

## Study session

God of all wisdom,
Help us to see and respond to truth
Wherever it is spoken or portrayed.

READINGS

1 Corinthians 13:8–12; John 18:32–38.

MEDITATIONS

'God ... is a God of surprises who supplies us with new insights into old truths and leads us into new paths of discovery, understanding and awareness.' (p. 105)

'We are not proclaiming good ideas. We are not purveyors of good advice. We are sharing good news based on truth revealed to us by God through Jesus Christ.' (p. 112)

'In the human family we are all partakers together in the search for a clearer understanding of God.' (p. 113)

'Since all truth is God's truth, Christians of all people need have no fear of truth wherever it is found.' (p. 117)

'God's order is important. Resurrection is only reached through the Cross.' (p. 123)

'If the Church is serious about effective mission it must be prepared to be exposed to the questions people ask.' (p. 125)

OUR EXPERIENCE

• 'People are the words with which God tells his story.' (p. 115) Share some of the people and situations which have expanded your understanding of God and God's world. (pp. 113–115)

• In our rapidly changing world, what are the new questions and challenges which we need to address and through which God might be speaking to us? (pp. 127ff.)

• What is, for you, the distinctive character of the truth which is summed up in Jesus Christ? (pp. 119–124)

CHRISTIAN RESPONSE

• 'The whole love of God can only be perceived in the whole people of God.' (p. 114) How might the diversity of Christian people help us to understand more of God's will and purpose for the whole world? How can distinctive gifts, personalities and experiences be best encouraged?

• 'There [are] not two kinds of truth – God's and some other kind. All truth is God's truth.' (p. 116) How does this insight assist the conversation between Christians and (for example) scientists, people of other faiths, psychologists and so on? What have we to offer and to learn in such dialogue?

• How is the balance between 'truth revealed' and 'truth discovered' (p. 111) to be described and maintained? Is the idea that truth is to be found in other faiths and life stances incompatible with Christian commitment to the Lordship of Christ? (pp. 119–120, 124ff.)

ACTION

• Invite a group of church and non-church people for a meal. Organise a sharing of convictions, stories and insights. What do we have in common? Where do we diverge? How can we better handle both?

• Propose three ways to increase 'grace and space' (pp. 124ff.) in your church.

• Compile a 'knowledge and experience' book for your study group. Put something in for everyone present. How can this information be used to advance your church's mission?

CLOSING PRAYER

God of mission and truth,
Maintain us in openness, conviction and discernment,
that we may discover your Way in all ways. Amen.

# 6

# 'Don't tell me – show me!'

## Mission is responding to human need wherever it is found

Jesus offered a succinct summary of the law of God. 'Love the Lord your God with all your heart, with all your soul, with all your mind and with all your strength', and 'Love your neighbour as yourself'. These are known as the two great commandments but actually they are one. They are inseparable. Our love for God is given substance in the love we have for others and the manner in which we serve their need. To pray 'Our Father in heaven' implies a relationship of love and service to our brothers and sisters on earth.

The purpose of this chapter is to probe the practical implications of that loving and serving relationship as a crucial component of our love for God and as an integral part of his mission to a complex and needy world. Essentially by 'need' we do not simply mean whatever people want or ask for. 'Need' is the need for whatever makes for full human flourishing in the image of God. As we will spell out more fully later in this chapter, it includes wholeness, fulfilment and participation.

It would be difficult to read the four gospel records of the life of Jesus without coming to the conclusion that he was just as interested in the practicalities of life as in the so-called spiritualities. Indeed, he didn't seem to draw any such distinction. There was, for him, a wholeness about life and he refused to break it up into separate, watertight compartments. For instance, it was entirely natural for him to include, at the very core of the prayer which he taught his disciples, a petition for daily bread. Bread took its rightful place alongside what some would consider weightier matters like forgiveness and temptation. Of course there was a deeper meaning included within that practical request, but we cannot escape from the basic truth it teaches us about God. He is not just interested in religion, he is interested in bread. Ordinary, everyday, practical matters, to do with our life in the world, are part of his concern. And, if we are serious about mission, they must become part of our concern also. People are not 'souls with ears' into which we are required to pour either our good news or our good advice. They are our brothers and sisters. Like us, they are made in the image of God. Wherever circumstances threaten to deny or diminish that image we, as partners in the mission of God, are not simply to decry such things. We are to challenge and confront them in the name of Jesus Christ and, whenever possible, convey practical help to those who are in need of it. Obedience to our Lord's command to love our neighbour involves us in serving them.

## I am among you as one who serves

Jesus led by example in this matter and, through his words and actions, left little room for his followers to evade the challenge. The story of the Good Samaritan[1] is a case in point. Here a detractor of Jesus attempts to evade the challenge of love by pressing for a precise definition – 'Who is my neighbour?' By doing so he tried to place limitations on his love and service towards those in need. He saw it in terms of selection and choice. He would decide who his neighbour was. Jesus made it clear in his reply that the man concerned, a lawyer by profession, was asking the wrong question. It was a matter neither of definition nor of selection. Rather, it was one of attitude and openness. The real question, contained in the penultimate punch line of the story, was 'To whom am I a neighbour?'

Part of the challenge emerging from that story, and encapsulated in the instruction from Jesus to the lawyer, was 'Go and do likewise'. It is a challenge not without its contemporary application. Am I prepared to cease from self-interest and calculated selection in my choice of those to whom I will be a neighbour? Am I prepared to flout convention, take risks, and be sacrificially generous, in order to bring help to those who are in genuine need? Though it is usually unwise to press the detail of a story of this kind it may not be totally insignificant to note that the good neighbour, the Samaritan, seemed to spare the victim the benefit of sound words and, instead, spent his energy and his money on sound and practical pastoral care!

The principle illustrated in the story was practised by Jesus throughout his ministry. 'I am among you as one who serves'[2] was a manifesto he clothed in flesh. People in need had a prior claim upon his time and energy. He was forever turning away from the curiosity of the multitude to the individual in practical need and distress. In the midst of the jostling crowds he was able to discern the tentative touch of faith of one who was at her wits end. He gave sight to one born blind and then slipped quietly away so that the man didn't even know who had healed him.[3]

But the classic example of the principle of service was demonstrated by Jesus in the presence of his disciples on the floor of the upper room. What they had steadfastly refused to do for him, that is, perform the common courtesy and wash the dust from his feet, he, in complete humility, did for them. After supper he took a towel, wrapped it round himself and, with a basin of water by his side, knelt on the floor and proceeded to wash the feet of his disciples. He took the place of a servant, put himself in a position where others could look down on him with contempt, and scraped the dirt from their feet. 'In the kingdom of God, service is not a stepping stone to nobility: it IS nobility, the only kind of nobility that is recognised.'[4] The insignia of the Kingdom of God is not crowns and coronets, but towels and basins.

Having washed their feet, Jesus relentlessly pressed home the message. 'Do you understand what I have done for you? You call me "Teacher" and "Lord", and rightly so, for that is what I am. Now that I, your Lord and Teacher, have washed your feet, you also should wash one another's feet. I have set you an example, that you should do as I have done to you.'[5]

There were two realities in that upper room. The one was symbolised in the towel and the basin. The other was symbolised in the bread and the cup. They point to the same truth. The service he rendered to his disciples on the floor was a microcosm of the deeper service he performed for humanity on the Cross. The Son of Man came not to be served, but to serve, and to give his life a ransom for many.[6] Such was the extent of his love and service towards his neighbour. This is the way the master trod; should not his servants tread it still?

## Yes, but who is my neighbour?

Unlike the lawyer in the story above we mustn't fall into the attitude of being selective in our choice or narrow in our definition. To be a true neighbour will require a breadth of vision that will perceive need, even when it doesn't immediately scream to be noticed, and begin to respond to it with understanding, compassion, imagination and courage. And we must start by lifting our eyes up and over our present horizons towards a wider perspective than that usually associated with the term 'neighbour'. So often it is seen in terms of offering practical help to an individual acquaintance who may be in difficulty. It may include that, of course, but our understanding of 'neighbour' cannot and must not be limited to a purely individualistic concept.

This truth came home to me with incredible force when I became Bishop of Bradford. I discovered, almost immediately, that some seventy thousand Muslims, Sikhs and Hindus looked to me, as the leader of the Anglican Church in that community, to be their neighbour and their voice when they felt marginalised, disregarded and disadvantaged. The same was true for school teachers, and for those working amongst the vulnerable in deprived areas, when savage council cuts adversely affected inner-city schools together with workers and organisations in the voluntary sector. Neighbourliness in that context consisted not in mouthing patronising platitudes and saying (just before I was driven back to my large house in my large car) 'I understand how you feel'. Rather, it meant standing up and being counted alongside those who described themselves as voiceless, choiceless and powerless.

At that point I was forced to see 'neighbouring' in more than individualistic terms. Neighbours can be families, organisations, neighbourhoods, our local community, groups who are marginalised, our nation, other nations, people we know, people we don't know – even people we will never know! Being a true neighbour is responding to human need in whomsoever and wheresoever it is found. It is not an optional extra for Christians, as we have seen from the example set by Jesus, nor is it a purely Christian prerogative. As is apparent in the story of the Good Samaritan, being a neighbour cuts right across religious, social and sectarian boundaries.

I encountered a classic example of this at the time of the Bradford City fire disaster which happened at Valley Parade Football Stadium in May 1985. Immediately after the fire the local residents, who were mostly Asians, opened their homes and their hearts to many people who, although not physically injured, were somewhat traumatised by the horrendous event and were in need of a little help and comfort. At the time I recall that some people spoke of such basic acts of kindness in rather surprised tones and they went out of their way to congratulate the Asian community. But congratulations were neither necessary nor appropriate, as events subsequently proved. For when it fell to me to organise the memorial service, and some were suggesting that the service should have an entirely Christian content, the Asian community made its feelings known in no uncertain terms – and it was absolutely right to do so. Such feelings were expressed thus: 'The people who perished in the fire were our "neighbours" and we wish to be "neighbours" to them and to their families. The Bradford community, of which we are a part, has suffered greatly and we wish to express our sorrow and sense of loss and our solidarity in sympathy with those who mourn.' In other words, the Asian community had felt diminished as a result of a tragedy which had struck the 'host' community. It was natural, therefore, for them to respond to human need. The fact that they were Muslims, for instance, made no difference. Christianity does not have a monopoly on serving our neighbours. The concept was built into the law of God in the Old Testament and the prophet Micah summed it up superbly when he wrote and declared the mind of God, as follows: 'And what does the Lord your God require of you, but to act justly, to love mercy and to walk humbly with your God'.[7]

It is not without significance that two of the three essentials that God requires have to do with people. A humble walk with God and justice and kindness in our human relationships – like the two Great Commandments endorsed by Jesus – must not be separated. According to Micah the one thing that ultimately matters is our relationship with God, but the only true test we have of the reality of that relationship is the quality of the relationship we have with other people. This 'Magna Charta of prophetic religion',[8] though it refers specifically to our coming to God in worship, provides a simple but searching test of the essence of true neighbourliness. Am I just in all my dealings? Am I kind to all people? Am I living in a humble relationship with God? Micah challenges us, whoever we are, to an integrated spirituality where acting justly, loving tenderly and walking humbly with God combines personal, interpersonal and public relationships and structures. If we are serious about serving our neighbour there is no better foundation on which to build than the amazingly wise, perceptive and understanding words attributed to the prophet Micah. Here is the basis not only of true neighbourliness but, indeed, of true religion.[9]

RIGHT WHERE WE ARE

There is no need for us to go looking for people to whom we can be neighbours. Wherever we are, whether in urban, rural or surburban communities we are surrounded by people who need to be served as neighbours. At the heart of such service is love which, if it is true love and springs from God himself, will include actions that will help establish the conditions in which people's lives are made more whole, more fulfilling and more participatory.

Such a task and such a vision are as crucial and as necessary in the life of an economically privileged community as they are on socially deprived housing estates. From my own experience, the latter situation may produce problems, demands and challenges that are more immediate and seemingly more acute, but the privileged community will certainly not be without its share of pain, frustration and tragic circumstance. Indeed, its needs may be even more challenging because they often lie beneath the surface, unacknowledged and unresolved. Loneliness, for instance, is not limited to those who live in high-rise flats; some chronic forms of it are experienced in the midst of advantage and affluence.

The one aspect of being a member of the Church of England which I appreciate most is its tradition of offering pastoral care not only to its 'signed-up' members but also to all those who live and work within each parish, irrespective of who they are and what they believe. Having served in several different parishes I am only too well aware of the disadvantages as well as the advantages of such a system. But the one thing it stops me from doing, if I am being true to the Anglican ethos, as well as Kingdom theology, is withdrawing into a gathered church mentality and ministering only to the members, or potential members, of my congregation.

God has placed his Church in society for the sake of society – in other words, to bear witness by its life and values to the love of God, and to seek the transformation of society by the power and application of that love. Among the most cynical comments one still hears from the lips of some who are 'in the Church of England but not of it' is that 'The C of E is the best boat to fish from'. I don't know of a comment less loving and more offensive towards our neighbours than that! Of course we are to search for the lost and seek to bring to faith those within our communities. We have been called for such a task. And of course we are to build up in the faith those who name the name of Christ within our churches, so that they may be sent out into the community to live and work for him. But our commitment and responsibility as Christians, and not just Anglican Christians, surely doesn't end there. Certainly God's commitment doesn't! God's love for the people in society and in our local community, who may have no faith commitment, is no less than his love for those who claim to be his disciples. Such love, translated into action, will serve certain goals in the lives of people whatever their religious allegiance, or lack of it. Such love will serve humankind's basic need for three things in particular.

## Wholeness

God, I believe, longs for and works towards the experience of wholeness in all of his creation and certainly in men and women. The frequent occurrence of the Hebrew word *shalom* in the Old Testament and its equivalent in the New Testament is a clear indication of this desire. *Shalom* (peace) means more than a courteous, conventional greeting, or even absence of war. It conveys a sense of wholeness, of unity and harmony within oneself and with others and with God. It is seen as a gift from God and the outstanding characteristic of the Messianic Kingdom where swords will be beaten into ploughshares and spears into pruning hooks. The disorder of nature will be dispelled. The enmity between humankind will disappear.

The content of the word *shalom* covers well-being in the widest sense of the word and includes prosperity, contentedness, bodily health, good relations between nations and people, and salvation. It has a social dimension and a public significance far beyond the purely personal, yet it also describes the person who lives his life in the 'presence' of God and is, therefore, 'fulfilled' or 'complete'.

Jesus clearly expressed this desire for and worked towards this *shalom* in his dealings with people. They had bodies to be healed as well as souls to be saved, sins to be forgiven as well as fears to be removed; they had emotions to be stirred as well as wills to be challenged; they had social obligations as well as religious commitments. One of the hallmarks of the life of Jesus was integration. It is recorded that 'He grew in wisdom and stature and in favour with God and men' (Luke 2:22). That is, physically, mentally, socially and spiritually he developed towards an integrated wholeness. It is a pattern which God would see developed in all of us. It is a pattern unlikely to be achieved to perfection in the lifetime of any of us but it is one towards which we must work, with the help of God, in our own lives and in the lives of people within our community.

This may mean, metaphorically speaking, getting our hands dirty as we struggle with people and institutions of power and influence in order to establish the social conditions in which people have a chance to become more whole. As I write this chapter the results of research have been published which indicates that those who live in socially deprived areas are more unhealthy and are more prone to life-threatening diseases and, therefore, are more likely to die earlier than others. This is but one instance. There are dozens of other circumstances in every community which serve to diminish rather than develop wholeness. Serving our neighbour in such circumstances requires us to work and speak with courage and determination for a change in a social environment which seems to prevent individuals, groups and whole communities from growing towards a greater wholeness.

It is surely instructive as well as interesting that the healing miracles of Jesus often crossed barriers to the outcast and the untouchable (the leper, the woman with the discharge of blood, the dead body, for example). Old Testament law excluded such people. Jesus' healings demonstrated that God includes society's outcasts.

*Shalom* or wholeness is indeed a gift from God but that does not excuse us from praying, working and crossing barriers in the name of God to enable *shalom* to be experienced in the lives of all people.

### Fulfilment

As we noted in an earlier chapter, it seems to be God's method to work from form to fullness. The Christian is described as one who is growing up into Christ. There is a sense of progress and development. Even creation is portrayed as moving towards completion and fulfilment.[10] A vital part of our growth towards wholeness as persons is a sense of fulfilment, the knowledge that we have God-given potential that needs to be realised rather than wasted; the conviction that we have a contribution to make to the life of the society in which we live and the local community of which we are a part.

Recently I visited a community centre in Southwark of which I am a patron. The occasion was the AGM at which a presentation of the work of the centre was to be given. It was hoped that my presence would be an encouragement to the members. During that visit I felt the Kingdom of God drawing very close to me and wasn't surprised, therefore, when my expectations were turned upside-down! I went to encourage; instead I was encouraged and inspired as people, young and old, spoke of discovering for the first time that they had potential and were given help to realise it not only for their own benefit but for the benefit of the local community. Many of the people concerned had been written off by society, by their families, by themselves. For some, life had been one long period of failure, frustration and rejection. Yet, there they were, with a developing confidence, standing before their peers and sharing the joy of fulfilment, with a humbling sense of genuine amazement that they had achieved something which other people valued. What was even more wonderful was the spontaneous pleasure with which their peers responded to the presentation by their friends. I found the whole occasion most moving. Here was a work of transformation. Here was mission in practical terms.

And it was not an isolated or unique event. It is happening right across the country and it needs to be encouraged more and more. People are the greatest resource in every community and the Church, if it is to serve its neighbour in practical and life-enhancing ways, needs to be involved in, or to pioneer, such efforts which so reflect the purpose of God for his human creatures and for the whole of his creation. The need for fulfilment in life is deep-seated and God-given. Those of us who are blessed with such a sense of fulfilment cannot rest easy while large groups within our society are deprived of it.

## Participation

Such fulfilment is more likely to be experienced in a community which has developed a participatory ethos. Where people's natural gifts and innate skills are recognised, enabled and deployed there is greater possibility for increasing wholeness and fulfilment among individuals and groups.

But it doesn't just happen by accident. It requires vision, courage and determination. All too often people find themselves excluded from that decision-making process which radically affects their way of life. Others make choices on their behalf, frequently without either consultation or accountability. Policies are implemented, sometimes in a politically doctrinaire manner, and those on the receiving end feel totally powerless in the matter. I am not just thinking of national or local government policies. The same thing happens away from the world of politics, in local groups, institutions, organisations – and in the Church. Our society is littered with people who feel 'shut out'. The advantages of the so-called 'good life' are presented to them *ad nauseam* in party political broadcasts, in television commercials, in glossy magazines and even from popular pulpits. But this only adds to their conviction that they are 'the shut-out ones' of society. Not only are they excluded from decision-making but their abilities and skills are unsought and unused in the building up of community life. They have so much to offer but receive so little encouragement and opportunity to do so.

One of my favourite Bible stories concerns Bartimaeus, the blind beggar encountered by Jesus on the Jericho road.[11] I particularly warm to it because of the insight it gives into the sensitive mind of God as revealed in Jesus. In that amazing incident Jesus refuses to do the expected thing and, without a by-your-leave, give Bartimaeus back his sight. It seemed the obvious thing to do, so why not get on and do it? Most of us probably would have done so, but not Jesus. He had the sensitivity to realise that to give sight to a blind beggar would cause a complete reorientation of his way of life. Having previously begged for a living, he would in future have to work for it and, as a result, his social relationships would be dramatically affected. It was not a moment to walk over a person's sensibilities with hob-nailed boots. Instead, Jesus recognised the human dignity of the beggar and consulted him about his own future. 'What do you want me to do for you?' he asked the blind beggar. Bartimaeus was given a voice and a choice regarding the direction and content of his future life. He chose wisely and well, received his sight and went on his way rejoicing and fulfilled.

I saw exactly the same principle being applied in the midst of social deprivation on an inner-city housing estate. The church held the vision of a self-help group of local residents providing a service for themselves and their neighbours. But the vision wasn't imposed upon local people. Instead, they were consulted. Their voices were heard and heeded. They were allowed to 'own' the vision. Their gifts and skills were affirmed and applied. They identified a derelict shop as the focus of their activities and the practical help they wished to offer to the neighbourhood. The church and the local authority combined as neighbours in providing the resources to refurbish the shop as a social centre so that local people could become neighbours to their own community of need. It was effective partnership and participation. It was frontline mission.

## Something of value to offer

The local church, because of its unique position within the community, as instanced in the situation described above, has a vital part to play in helping to establish the conditions in which people's lives are made more whole, more fulfilling and more participatory.

The Church, of course, must always maintain a proper attitude of humility. It has nothing that it has not received from God. It must pray, therefore, to be delivered from foolish pride. But, equally, it must not succumb to false modesty. God has given it certain gifts and many advantages when it comes to serving its neighbourhood.

We are living in a society where, increasingly, there is a shrinking voluntary sector, a growing upward and outward social mobility, and the emergence of 'sink' estates with their downward spiral of deprivation and demoralisation. In such a situation the Church is often the only remaining organisation which is 'multi-activity'. No longer are churches open only on Sunday. Greater and greater numbers of them are in business seven days a week and provide a whole variety of activities for the benefit of the local community. The Church in very many communities is the only remaining organisation which has building plant for community use, a team of volunteers to 'keep the show on the road', and a paid staff, highly trained and locally resident. Often the Church is the only remaining organisation which is multi-age and multi-cultural. Its membership spans all ages and transcends all cultures. It is the only organisation of which claims can be made to serve your neighbour and which has a long and proven record of advocacy and service delivery. The Church is ideally placed, divinely called and comparatively well-equipped to serve its neighbour. The fact that it also has individual representatives scattered throughout society, together with a corporate national network with an ecumenical dimension, only increases its opportunities for offering service to those in need.

There are two other particular services of importance which the Church can offer its local or national community. First of all the Church can help and encourage the community to celebrate its diversity. This is not as theoretical or as idealistic as it may sound. Many people take an extremely negative view of diversity. They see it as threatening and are fearful of it. They respond by keeping themselves to themselves. All too often the unfortunate next step is to stereotype those who are different from them, because of language, colour or social standing, and so there develops an atmosphere of suspicion and mistrust which, in certain circumstances, can degenerate into conflict. The term 'multi-cultural' needs to be used accurately and with care. Sadly, it is sometimes used in a derogatory manner as a kind of misfortune that has overtaken us. What a travesty!

Diversity, of which the multi-cultural is an important dimension, is not something to be openly denigrated or reluctantly tolerated, rather it is to be joyfully celebrated. We need to take pleasure in and affirm the richness and variety of the communities we serve. Sometimes the Church has been so eager to emphasise the coherent unity of God's creation that it has failed to celebrate the exuberant diversity of the world and its people. This note of joy for diversity is particularly present in Celtic spirituality where there is a strong element of praise and thanksgiving that God, far from making the world uniform, has endowed it with a creative variety that calls for celebration.

Secondly, within that diversity that we celebrate, we can serve our community by listening to the cry of those caught up in situations of powerlessness and poverty. The constant refrain that one hears in working with ordinary people, especially in deprived urban areas, is that no one really listens to them. Talking recently to a residents' group on one of our most demoralised estates, I found their feelings were summed up in these words: 'All kinds of people come and talk to us, they take notes of what we say, they utter sympathetic noises, they even promise to do something to help solve our problems. But we have heard it all before. Nothing happens – until the next time, when a new group of people come and we have a repeat performance. No one actually listens, that is, no one pays attention to what we are saying.'

Serving and loving our neighbour in such circumstances demands that we get to grips with that kind of problem. Love is paying attention. Love is hearing and heeding the cry of the poor in such situations. Love is becoming the voice of the poor to those who need to hear and have the resources to respond to their cry. Love in this sense is very practical. It involves actions as well as words. It cannot be expressed in 'spiritual' terms. James expresses this truth in fairly stark and challenging manner: 'Suppose a brother or sister is without clothes and daily food. If one of you says to him, "Go, I wish you well; keep warm and well fed", but does nothing about his physical needs, what good is it? In the same way, faith by itself, if it is not accompanied by action, is dead.' (James 2:15–17)

'An intrinsic part of knowing God is loving, and fighting for the cause of, our neighbour.'[12] It is not a matter of paternalism. Christian love is much more than paternalism to the poor. It is intent on restoring to the poor what rightly belongs to them. It is not just concerned with being a voice for the poor – though that may of necessity be required in the short term – it is more concerned with giving the poor back their voice so that they can become the agents and bearers, and not just the objects, of mission.

Indeed, as we shall note a little later in this chapter, we must be sensitive in 'serving' our neighbour lest we give the impression that we are 'doing' something to them, thus making them 'victims'. As Henri Nouwen reminds us, 'The Spirit of love is hidden in their poverty, brokenness and grief'.[13] In the long run, mission is possible only when it is as much receiving as giving, as much being cared for as caring. The amazing story of The Sheep and The Goats told by Jesus in Matthew 25 illustrates the same truth in a most dramatic fashion. As we reach out to serve others in the name of Jesus we discover him reaching out to us through them. There is a mutuality of giving and receiving. We receive from those to whom we are sent.

## Reversing the destiny of the poor

Both Old and New Testaments express a profound concern for 'the poor'. In Law and Prophets, in Psalms and Proverbs, God, it seems, reveals what has been called 'a preferential option for the poor'.[14] We must not interpret this in terms of God favouring the poor at the expense of the rich, for God has no favourites. Rather, it is God redressing the imbalance that has arisen whereby the rich have become richer at the expense of the poor.

So God provides laws that are geared to curb those who would oppress the poor. He requires of the king, who is his representative, that he exercises his authority to protect the poor and in doing so to reveal the very nature of God himself. He asks for justice, mercy and tenderness in our relationships with each other rather than exploitation, vindictiveness and harshness.[15] He indicates that the poor can expect to be shown his grace while the rich will incur judgement if they fail to exhibit the spirit of dependence revealed in the lives of the poor they are exploiting.

The theme is continued throughout the New Testament and particularly in the life and ministry of Jesus who, significantly, chose not only to be born into a poor family but also to live in relative poverty for the whole of his earthly life. He chose to identify with the poor and, like them, suffered deprivation, hatred, rejection and homelessness, on the margins of society.

Supremely, he saw his task in terms of reversing the

destiny of the poor. That, I believe, was the whole point of his programmatic sermon in the synagogue at the beginning of his ministry:

> The Spirit of the Lord is upon me,
> because he has anointed me
> to preach good news to the poor,
> He has sent me to proclaim freedom for the prisoners
> and recovery of sight for the blind,
> to release the oppressed,
> to proclaim the year of the Lord's favour.[16]

The prisoners, the blind, the oppressed are all subsumed under 'the poor'. They are all the 'excluded' or 'shut-out ones' and as such are in need of good news. And the good news is that Jesus has been chosen and empowered by God to reverse their destiny so that they are no longer pushed to the margins of society. Contained within the words 'the year of the Lord's favour' is a reference to the Year of Jubilee legislation, the intention of which was to ensure the eventual lifting of the burdens of the poor and impoverished.

However, it seems that the power of the wealthy in Israel was sufficient to frustrate the experience of Jubilee. 'The Jubilee trumpet never sounded. But Jesus resurrected the Jubilee provision and brought it from the level of theory to the level of practice.'[17] He did what the religious leaders of his day failed to do. He proclaimed the year of the Lord's favour and he gave it substance. No, he didn't end the sufferings of all the oppressed, nor did he cancel the debts of all who were in hock to the rich. But he gave tangible evidence of what he could do. He transformed the life of a tax collector, Matthew, and made him one of his disciples. He so radically changed the life of Zacchaeus that he gave back to the poor all that he had fraudulently extracted from them. 'And all over Palestine there were families who rejoiced because a child was alive who had been dead, because a blind man could see, because a cripple could walk. And the religious and the rich began to tremble over a Man who had reminded them of the divine law!'[18]

This is the good news at the heart of all true mission. It is certainly what the Church is sent into the world to do, and included within it is the call to love, to serve, to preach, to teach, to heal, to liberate. As Professor Moltman wrote, such mission 'embraces all activities that serve to liberate men and women from their slavery in the presence of the coming God, slavery which extends from economic necessity to Godforsakenness'.[19]

Reversing the destiny of the poor is not optional for a Church which is called to 'serve your neighbour'. 'Once we recognise the identification of Jesus with the poor, we cannot any longer consider our own relation to the poor as a social ethics question; it is a gospel question.'[20] If that is so, and I believe it is, the Church is left with no choice but to identify with the poor. But it requires courage – and it is costly.

CONFRONTING INJUSTICE

Identification with the poor cost Jesus his life. If the Church is to identify effectively with the poor, there is a price to pay. There will be times when it will be misunderstood and criticised by its own members for doing so. At other times it will incur the wrath of local and national politicians and its actions and viewpoints will be dismissed with disdain. It is not an arena for faint hearts.

I vividly recall standing in that arena on one occasion, having confronted a local authority with what I considered its unjust dealings with the poor. There was little doubt that the Church occupied the moral high ground in the debate. There was a clear conviction that the Church was voicing the genuine concerns of those being further marginalised by council policy. But the politicians felt threatened by it and when three of them came to see me and my two colleagues they, metaphorically, wiped the floor with us. They didn't win the argument. They couldn't. But they employed the classic tactic of 'shouting louder'. They were aggressive in their blitz-like attack and they were happy to ignore the Marquis of Queensberry rules! My colleagues and I couldn't match them. It wasn't that we hadn't done our homework or that we didn't have right on our side. We were simply too nice. We played it the Christian way – and they walked all over us. And in doing so they taught us a lesson. If the Church is going to 'mix it' with people who have power and don't wish to share it, it will need to put on the whole armour of God and, to the equipment listed in the letter to the Ephesians,[21] it may need to add an abundant supply of 'godly belligerence'!

We need to remember the anger of prophets like Amos in the face of injustice. He stood up and was counted on the issue. He confronted it with vehemence. He recognised that social institutions were promoting injustice and that even religious institutions had become hijacked for political ends – and he didn't mince his words in response. He believed that God was the sovereign Lord of all, that all human beings were precious to God, and called for justice 'to roll down like waters, and righteousness like an ever flowing stream' (Amos 5:24). Amos was not a lone voice. His fellow prophets also spoke out against injustice. They were prepared to condemn the extremes of wealth that forced poverty on others. They didn't just sympathise with those in need, they spoke against the perpetrators of oppression. Compassion for the oppressed and anger against the oppressor seems to be a consistent message emerging from the Old Testament. It is certainly the under-lying truth that is portrayed in the story of the Exodus. Even a gentle soul like the Blessed Virgin Mary said some fairly straight and revolutionary things on this particular subject in her Magnificat: 'He has brought down rulers from their thrones but has lifted up the humble. He has filled the hungry with good things but has sent the rich away empty.'[22]

FACING THE FACTS

We may argue until the cows come home as to what consti-tutes 'the poor' in today's society. We may spend time making comparisons with days gone by, when we were young. We may allow ourselves to be distracted by those who unfairly want either to blame the poor by saying 'it's their own fault', or to class them all as 'those who want to claim their rights but are not willing to make any useful contribution to the life of their community'. But we would be foolish to ignore the fact that there are millions of people in our own land, to say nothing of other parts of the world, who are poor and becoming poorer every day.

Materially, sociologically and politically they feel deprived. They see themselves dismissed to the margins of our contemporary society and allowed little or no partici-pation in it. It is a marginality that comprises all spheres of life and is often so extensive that people feel they have no resources to do anything about it. They are shut out. The door is closed. And they have no power to open it. They feel themselves to be the victims of society. We might believe, or wish, that it were otherwise. But it is not. We might also make the mistake of limiting 'the poor' to deprived urban areas. Again we would be foolish to do so. They can often be found in rural areas, in county towns and hidden away in suburbia. Poverty is no respecter of persons or communities. The poor are a fact of modern life.

The Church at both national and local level, if it is going to be a good neighbour to the poor, will need to identify areas of injustice that are seriously affecting people's lives – whether in the realms of employment, housing and health, or in matters of equal opportunities, racism and sexuality – and confront them in the name of the God of justice. We must not be afraid of 'mixing it' with politicians, legislators and those who exercise power and influence in our society. The Church must believe that it is as 'spiritual' to work for the social cohesion of our community as it is to evangelise it and that we have a major contribution to make to the former as well as to the latter.

Theology and ethics belong together. You can't have one without the other. God, as he has revealed himself through scripture and in Jesus, requires justice in all our dealings, whether in private life or in public responsibilities. As we have already noted, the Old Testament law is summarised in the command to love God and to love our neighbour. The law, in other words, reflects the character of God and demonstrates a pattern of life appropriate for human beings made in God's image. The social and political expression of neighbour love is justice – and that relates as much to social systems as to personal values. If we are on the side of God we have no option but to be on the side of the poor also. That commits us not only to pray but also to work and legislate for justice. It is not enough to seek the transformation of the individual; we must also work to change unjust structures into structures of grace.

A NOTE OF CAUTION

It would be a travesty, as I mentioned earlier, if in our emphasis on God's 'preferential option for the poor' we gave the least impression that he had little time for the rich. That would be a gross distortion. It simply isn't true. During his ministry Jesus was happy to talk to the rich as well as the poor and he made friends with both. It is clear from the New Testament that many people of material substance became followers and disciples of Jesus. Some of the wealthiest people in today's society are committed to Christ and to the values and standards of his Kingdom. The scriptures neither glorify poverty nor condemn wealth, and nor must we. The love of God is not limited to the poor. When the rich young ruler came to Jesus looking for the secret of how he might inherit eternal life, our Lord's love for him was deep and genuine.[23]

I believe that our Lord was concerned to show that the rich as well as the poor needed a neighbour. Just as the poor were forced by circumstances to be dependent on the grace of God so also the rich needed to be helped towards the same attitude. How else can we understand our Lord's response to the rich young ruler – 'Go and sell everything you have and give it to the poor and come take up the cross and follow me'? It sounds fairly drastic stuff and it needs to be put in perspective because Jesus didn't make such demands of every would-be disciple. He called both rich and poor to follow him but his message for the rich was different from the one he gave the poor.

Jesus was replying to the young man's desire to be told what he must do to inherit eternal life. So he simply took him at his word and, putting his finger on the sore spot, challenged him in the most radical and demanding way about his love for God. Deep down in the heart of the young man there was obviously a clash of loyalties and a conflict of loves – on the one hand possessions and on the other hand God. They are not mutually exclusive. It is quite possible to be wealthy and godly, but it is quite impossible to be a servant of both. Jesus loved the young man and wanted to be a true neighbour to him, so he didn't fudge the issue. You cannot serve God and mammon.

We serve our rich neighbours when we encourage and challenge them towards an attitude of dependence upon God rather than upon possessions. We serve them when we expound to them the standards of the Kingdom which requires that they serve the weak rather than gather more strength to themselves. We serve them when we inspire them, in their strength and with their influence, to become advocates for justice, voices for social change, and partners with the poor in the building of true community.

I have always been an admirer of William Wilberforce. His work as a Christian statesman and social reformer continues to be a source of inspiration, encouragement and example. We quite properly need to thank God for the breadth of his vision, the power of his oratory and the depth of his courage in seeking to alleviate poverty and curb disadvantage. He was a tireless worker and advocate for the poor. But therein, it seems, lay the one aspect of his work which we need not only to build upon but also to extend, namely, his relationship to the poor. Alex Vidler tells us that Wilberforce and the members of the Clapham Sect worked *for* the poor rather than *with* the poor.[24]

Today that emphasis needs to be changed. The rich need to follow the example of God himself in working *with* the poor in seeking the Kingdom of righteousness, justice and peace, the rich becoming neighbours to the poor, and the poor becoming neighbours to the rich, in an equal partnership for the benefit of all. There is an inclusiveness about such a partnership that reflects the inclusiveness of God and the gospel.

## A modern scourge

Such an inclusive partnership could become a powerful force against one of the greatest evils of our day, namely, racism. Far too many of our neighbours are the victims of this endemic and deplorable scourge. 'Racism is a form of poverty inflicted upon people':[25] that is, it diminishes, deprives and excludes them. It is a poison that has seeped into every aspect of life in contemporary society.

We see the public and unacceptable face of racism in the desecration of Jewish graves, in the daubing of offensive slogans on the walls of mosques, gurdwaras and temples and in the harassment continually directed against Asian and West Indian families in places like South London. We are conscious of a kind of institutional racism in connection with some aspects of immigration control and law enforcement. And when it comes to matters like employment, there is little doubt that young blacks find it infinitely more difficult to obtain work than their white peers.

But it is the incipient attitude that persists throughout society that is of deepest concern. That is the seed-bed in which racism grows. That is the backdrop against which racism is practised without, by and large, the widespread public condemnation it deserves. Ordinary people simply will not believe that they are guilty of racism until they are caused to pause and think about their attitudes, their words and their actions. And when they do, they are often shocked and shamed by what they discover about themselves. It is not a pleasant thing to discover that one has been 'programmed' by prejudice.

As a young Protestant boy from the back streets of Belfast I was programmed not to trust Catholics; to believe that you could always tell a Catholic by looking at his eyes; to consider all Catholics to be traitors and all Protestants to be loyal. Looking back it seems ludicrous that I could imbibe without question such unreasonable attitudes. But I can't deny facts. I had learned all too early in life, not from my parents I hasten to add, for I never heard a prejudicial whisper from either of them, but from the prevailing climate in that society, the deadly practice of stereotyping, the crippling sectarianism – and all the prejudice, intolerance, suspicion and fear that flowed from it.

We need to examine very carefully the attitudes we have towards black people and how those attitudes have developed. How much is founded on reality and how much on fantasy? Have we been programmed by the prevailing climate in society? How often have we challenged society's prejudices on the matter? Have we passively accepted the common view and, without realising it, become part of the vicious circle that perpetrates racism by doing nothing about it?

Our society needs neighbours. If it is to grow towards true health and wholeness it needs the help and courage of those who will resist, and keep on resisting, the perpetrators of this pernicious evil. Serving our neighbour in this particular context means becoming implacably opposed to words, actions and attitudes that are dismissive of those whose skin is a different colour from our own.

Most people are prepared to deplore excessive acts of racial violence which result in community disturbance. But more than this is needed. We need to become more actively involved in building bridges between people across the racial divide. Though few of us are prepared to admit it, most of us need help in recognising the innate racism that is in each of us. We need to set our faces against stereotyping. We need to speak out courageously whenever racist remarks are made in our company. There is a way of doing this without sounding prudish, though I don't think we should be too worried about causing embarrassment! We white people need to unlearn many of the things we think we know about black people or, at least, have the courtesy to check out our perceptions. We need to repent of past attitudes and actions and we need the humility to ask our black brothers and sisters for their help in getting it right in the future.

This is vital for the sake of society and, indeed, for our sake, whether we are black or white. We need each other. We have cultural riches to share with each other. If we fail to do so we deprive society and ourselves of greater growth towards maturity and completeness.

### Don't tell me – show me!

The Church must not only declare the need to love and serve our neighbour. It must also be prepared to demonstrate in every aspect of its own life the truth it proclaims. It must be seen to *do* the truth – that is, 'Faith active in love'.[26]

It is in this regard that the Church needs to receive service as well as offer it. In this sense the Church may need the help of a neighbour and the local community can offer that help by asking the right questions, if only the local church has the openness and the ability to hear them.

Such questions might take the following form: You speak of the vital importance of establishing conditions in which people's lives are made more participatory. Why, then, are so many of your worship services, because of their language and content, so inaccessible to the local community? You speak of the value of listening to those in need. What mechanisms do you have in the local church to ensure that you hear the authentic voice of the community and, especially, the cry of those who feel pushed to the margins? You encourage us to act against racism in society. What steps are you taking against racism in the Church? When there are so many black people in some congregations why are there comparatively few in positions of leadership? You plead for justice in society and suggest that we confront injustice wherever we find it. But what about the Church? Is it always just in its dealings? Aren't decisions which radically affect people's lives often taken without them being consulted? Does not the Church have 'power groups' that determine policy simply by the strength of their membership or by clever manipulation of the media? You say that God in his love accepts all. Why, then, does the Church frequently give the impression that some are more acceptable than others? You claim to be the Body of Christ in this neighbourhood. Are you aware of how you are perceived in the community and what message your building conveys? You extol the story of the Good Samaritan, but wasn't it the despised 'outsider' who came out best in that story? Hasn't the Church something to learn from those outside its structures?

I believe that the Church must address such questions with sensitivity and sincerity. In seeking to fulfil the command of Jesus to love our neighbour we need to acknowledge our own need of neighbourly help. Traditionally the Church has always worked from its strengths to others' weaknesses. We give. They receive. But in these days we need to develop a willingness to work from our weakness to others' weakness, sharing the same experience of powerlessness, being 'in the same boat', standing alongside. In humility we need to work from our weakness to the strengths of others, loving and affirming, encouraging and enabling them to share, and share again, their resources with their needy neighbours.

One of the lessons taught by Jesus in the upper room, on the night when he washed the feet of his disciples, was that you can only be a servant of others when you are prepared to let others be your servant. The Church will have greater integrity in serving its neighbour and inspiring others to do so when it recognises its own need of help. It is not without significance that the spirituality of Jesus was one of openness, honesty and vulnerability. A Church which follows his example will have no trouble in acknowledging its own inherent weaknesses and, therefore, be better equipped to help and be helped.

> Brother let me be your servant
> Let me be as Christ to you
> Pray that I may have the grace
> To let you be my servant too.

There is a risk in serving others and in allowing others to serve us. Love is at the heart of service and loving is a risky business. God's love for the world involved the risk and reality of a Cross. Our love for God and for our neighbour will involve risk – and, ultimately, who knows where it will lead? That is a topic we shall examine in the next and final chapter.

## Study session

OPENING PRAYER

> May Christ be the vision
> In the eyes that see us
> In the ears that hear us
> In the hearts that call us and
> In the hands that reach out to us.

READINGS

Micah 6:8; Luke 4:16–21.

MEDITATIONS

'God is not just interested in religion, he is interested in bread.' (p. 133)

Jesus says, 'I am among you as one who serves.' (p. 134)

'The insignia of the Kingdom of God is not crowns and coronets but towels and basins.' (p. 135)

'God, as revealed through scripture and in Jesus, requires justice in all our dealings whether in private life or public responsibilities.' (p. 154)

'Our Lord was concerned to show that the rich needed a neighbour as well as the poor.' (p. 155)

OUR EXPERIENCE (IN PAIRS)

• Who are the people in most need in our church, neighbourhood, nation? (Name some groups and people.)

• Think of a time when you or someone close to you has been vulnerable or needy. What have you wanted from others? What have you not wanted from them? (Compile two lists.)

• How does our church's existing programme of service match up to our answers to these questions? (Are we reaching out appropriately?)

CHRISTIAN RESPONSE (AS A GROUP)

• 'We serve our rich neighbours when we encourage and challenge them towards an attitude of dependence upon God rather than upon possessions.' (p. 156) 'Love is hearing and heeding the cry of the poor . . . Love is becoming the voice of the poor to those who need to hear and have the resources to respond.' (p. 148) Referring back to the biblical readings (pp. 137–138, 149–150), consider both the *gospel roots* of these two statements, and the *practical implications* for our Church's mission and ministry.

• Why is racism identified as such a crucial issue in serving our neighbour? (pp. 157–159)

• 'Traditionally the Church has always worked from its strengths to others' weaknesses. We give. They receive.' Does this accord with Jesus' model of service? How can it be changed?

• Look at the challenges to the Church (pp. 159–161). How would *you* answer them?


ACTION

• Consider a way of more effectively and practically 'heeding the cry of the poor' in our situation.

• In the light of our reflection, what should we be doing more of and less of as a Church?

CLOSING PRAYER

God of love,
Help us to match the praise of our mouths
with the tenderness of our hearts
and the justice of our deeds,
For Christ's sake. Amen.

# Catching up with God

Mission is following Jesus
in his suffering love
for the salvation of all people

Many bishops, following their enthronement service, process out of the west door of their Cathedral Church and symbolically bless the city. When I became Bishop of Bradford that particular convention wasn't expected of me, probably because the city couldn't be seen from the west door. However, as I walked back to the Provost's house to unrobe, it was just possible to glimpse a little bit of the city over my left shoulder. In the forefront of my view were three shops: the first, a coffee shop, the second, a Unit Trust office and the third, a betting shop. The first spoke of fellowship, the second of security and the third of risk. The scene struck me as a kind of parable regarding the shape of my future ministry. Fellowship and security might be desirable but I was more interested in the risk involved in mission. By risk I mean not the foolhardiness of the adventurer simply out to make a name for myself, but rather the moral courage to place ourselves at the disposal of God even when the odds and the opinions of others are against us. The fellowship and security of belonging to Christ and his Church is a wonderful privilege, but as followers of Jesus we are also called to a ministry of risk and adventure in pursuing the mission of God which has, as its ultimate goal, the salvation of all people.

Jesus himself seemed to be clear about this point when he commissioned the seventy disciples, 'Go, I am sending you out as lambs among wolves' (Luke 10:3). There was clearly nothing secure or comfortable in that prospect. It was certainly a little risky for the lambs! And modern-day followers of Jesus who are prepared to move out in mission from the privileged fellowship and secure belonging of their local church will soon discover that the analogy of the lambs and the wolves is not as far-fetched as some would imagine. Confronted by the chill winds of secularism, materialism, some aspects of post-modernity, and the widespread unbelief that pervades many of our national and social institutions, they will soon bear witness to the feeling of being like vulnerable lambs in the midst of devouring wolves.

Following Jesus in his sacrificial love was a risky business in the Early Church. It still is today – though the risks are of a different calibre and the wolves are not always immediately recognisable. In this chapter we will look at the risk that was part of the life and ministry of Jesus and we will consider what it means to follow Jesus in his suffering love today. We will look at some of the worthwhile risks that need to be taken as the Church moves in mission towards and into the third millennium and we will examine what salvation means in such a context.

## Continue and complete

There is no better place to start than in the upper room with the risen Lord as he commissions his disciples to continue and complete the mission which he had begun. 'As the Father has sent me, I am sending you' (John

20:21).[1] Forty times in this Gospel Jesus is described as the one sent by the Father. Here he is the one who sends others to fulfil the task he had inaugurated. But his integrity is such that he makes it clear that there is a risk involved in going. His words are prefaced by a powerful and dramatic visible sign: 'He showed them his hands and his side.' Here was a stark demonstration that it was a risky occupation to be a follower of his. The scars of crucifixion and death that he revealed in his hands and side were not only proofs of his identity; they indicated a cost to be expected by those whom he commissions. 'As the Father has sent me, I am sending you.'

Their mission is the same as his. Like his, it is a mission involving costly identification with those he came to serve and save. It is a mission of self-emptying and humble service. It is a mission which inevitably includes risk. How could it be otherwise when at its heart there is a cradle and a Cross? It is so easy, especially at an emotive time like Christmas, to portray the Incarnation in such glowingly sentimental terms as to omit any reference to the risk factor that was involved in such an event. But when God became human he also became vulnerable, if one dare speak of God in such terms. God in Christ was subject to all the vicissitudes of life – including death. God was in Christ reconciling the world to himself and in doing so experienced weariness, frustration, homelessness, rejection, failure and crucifixion. The Cross did not take God by surprise. The cradle made the Cross inevitable. The risk involved in the former led, inexorably, to the latter. The old priest Simeon gave Mary a strong hint of this at the time when she and Joseph presented the baby Jesus in the temple. 'This child is destined to cause the falling and rising again of many in Israel, and to be a sign that will be spoken against. And a sword will pierce your own heart too.' (Luke 2:34–35) Over the joy of his birth there lay the shadow of his death.

From the time he was born in a stable to the time he was raised from the dead he faced risk of one kind or another. He escaped from the murderous intentions of Herod. He endured the blood, sweat and tears of vulnerable ministry. He was betrayed by friends and opposed by foes. He was falsely accused by religious leaders, unjustly executed by the civil authority and, surprisingly, on the Cross experienced being forsaken by God, his Father. Small wonder he built an element of risk into the job description of his followers when he said, 'If anyone would come after me, he must deny himself and take up his cross. For whoever wants to save his life will lose it, but whoever loses his life for me will find it.' (Matthew 16:24–25)

Risk was part and parcel of the life of Jesus and those who follow him today are unlikely to avoid it. Indeed, the refusal to take risks is the refusal to have faith. There is risk in following Jesus because we are never quite sure where it will end. But we know it will result in self-giving for that is the essence of suffering love.

## Beyond the fringe

Following Jesus in his suffering love will take us to some surprising places to meet some surprising people and to grasp some surprising opportunities. No one can read the parable of The Sheep and The Goats[2] without being struck by the element of surprise surrounding the whereabouts of Jesus in the lives and circumstances of certain people. Those who expressed practical love for the prisoner, the sick and the destitute were vastly surprised to learn that in doing so they were ministering to Jesus. Clearly, he was

there before them. Conversely, those who failed or refused
to offer practical service to such unfortunate people were
shaken to discover that they had been withholding help and
love from that same Jesus.

Truly, Jesus not only comes to his Church in word and
sacrament where, so often, we behold him in glory and
worship him, but he also awaits his Church in the unlikely
places and people where, in the midst of their suffering
and distress, we behold him in brokenness and serve him.
Following Jesus in his suffering love today will include such
surprises and opportunities beyond the fringe of normal
church life and activity.

All too often, however, we read this most challenging,
indeed, terrifying, parable without allowing it to impact
seriously upon our church policy at the local and national
level. Where are today's 'unlikely' places and who are
today's 'unlikely' people to which and to whom Jesus has
gone before and calls us to follow? It is a question we
constantly need to be asking. It requires a discernment for
which we need the help of God's Spirit.

Written indelibly on my heart in this regard is an experience I had as a young vicar in Nottingham in the early
seventies. The large parish for which I was responsible was
part of a massive slum clearance project. Virtually the whole
area was being demolished and rebuilt and some fairly
militant and very vociferous groups were formed to ensure
that their particular view would be heard and their demands
met. The advice that many of my evangelical friends gave
me was to keep out of politics, concentrate on building my
new church and leave the rest to God. The advice seemed
sensible and sound, but it was flawed. To have followed it
would have made life a little easier in the short term, but I
wouldn't have had the surprise of discovering God in the
midst of all the hassle, frustration, blood, sweat and tears
of a community struggling for what we Christians call

*shalom*. Most of the members of the local pressure groups would not have had the full biblical content of that word in mind in their political activism. But I have little doubt that in their own way they were striving towards a state of affairs that would produce a well-being within the community that was part of the *shalom* of God.

I have to confess that at times it was both agonising and demoralising to be involved in trying to build community where pressure groups vied with each other for power, where Christian standards were not overtly applied and where the atmosphere at public meetings was at times hostile and destructive. There were times when, like the psalmist, I longed 'for wings like a dove that I might fly away and be at rest' (Psalm 55:6). But to have stood aloof from such a struggle would, I believe, not only have been a betrayal of the community but also a denial of the gospel of love, peace and justice. It would also have been a refusal to follow Jesus in his suffering love. I could not but believe that God was present in a work of urban regeneration that sought to transform the life of a community. It seemed important, therefore, to catch up with God by getting involved – even if it meant going beyond the fringe of the Church and my own previous experience.

As matters worked out, the Church's contribution to the debate and the fact that it had identified with the struggle and hopes of the local people, had very considerable influence on the outcome for the good of the whole community. As a result, the well-being of a regenerated community was enhanced and the continuing presence of the Church within it was stamped with an integrity which served to make its witness more effective.

## Across the frontiers

Following Jesus in his suffering love will not only take us beyond the fringe of church life it will also carry us across frontiers in society.

While on earth Jesus was almost always to be found on those frontiers. He was prepared to challenge the establishment, to keep company with the vulnerable, to confront the boundaries of prejudice and to build and cross bridges of understanding and reconciliation. He was driven towards and across those frontiers by a burning and compassionate love for people. That love constrained him to set aside convention and custom if these things got in the way of grace and mercy, forgiveness and justice.

Today's disciples must be prepared to follow in his footsteps towards today's frontiers, which are both numerous and complex – some would even say dangerous. Take, for instance, the matter of inter-faith co-operation and dialogue which I mentioned in an earlier chapter. There is little doubt in my own mind that in the early years of the third millennium this matter will assume even greater significance in the life of the nation and present a massive challenge to the Church. Yet, although there are notable exceptions, most Christians are content, indeed relieved, to leave inter-faith issues to other people, to those who 'like that sort of thing'. There is an anxiety lest in following the example of such people we get 'out of our depth' and have to struggle to survive in maintaining our own faith.

In this matter, as in so many others, the example of Jesus in crossing frontiers is worth following. I refer in particular to his encounter with the woman at the well of Samaria.[3] Here Jesus not only crosses the sexual frontier, or barrier, that existed in Jewish custom between men and women, he was also prepared to cross the racial, and sometimes hostile, frontier between Samaritan and Jew. He even went a step further by asking a kindness of the woman, thus making himself vulnerable by placing himself in her debt. During their conversation he doesn't 'pull rank' by trying to control the situation. Instead he allows her to direct matters, taking the conversation where she will, while he with the utmost courtesy responds to her agenda.

It is a classic incident and one which repays careful study for the considerable guidance and insight it gives regarding inter-faith dialogue. But my reason for mentioning it here is to stress that in following Jesus in his suffering love we must be prepared to cross frontiers into territory that may be threatening and uncomfortable and where we may feel very exposed and vulnerable. It may involve us in flouting convention. It may result in misunderstanding on the part of our friends – not an uncommon experience for Jesus – and it may cause us personal anxiety lest we should be perceived as 'letting the side down'!

I remember such feelings crowding in upon me on three specific occasions. The first was in a Hindu temple when, as a special guest, I sat with a garland round my neck, next to the Elephant God, and addressed the assembled company. As graciously as I could I identified some of the differences between Christians and Hindus as well as some of the common factors. Though I was in the midst of many gracious Hindu friends I felt very isolated. The second was in a Sikh gurdwara when I again had the privilege of speaking to the worshippers and performing the equivalent of giving out the Sunday school prizes! The third occasion was a national Muslim rally when I sat on a platform with eleven Muslim leaders and was asked to address over one thousand people in an atmosphere that was fairly volatile. I was not expected to be unduly accommodating to my hearers but to address their Muslim concerns from a Christian perspective. It was a thrilling, terrifying and very lonely assignment.

On each of these occasions I felt cut off from my fellow Christians – and some of them by their subsequent attitude confirmed my feelings as correct! Yet it seemed to me that in following Jesus in his suffering love for the salvation of all people I might fully expect to be taken to places, people and experiences where I had never been before. Is not this of the essence of mission?

## Across boundaries

Mission will not only require us to move beyond the fringe and across the frontiers, it will also demand that we cross boundaries that have become restrictive, into a freedom that enables us to explore the relevance of the gospel for a new age, with new knowledge and new challenges, some of which may be quite disturbing in their implications. This is particularly the case in the field of business, medical and personal ethics.

It may be perfectly possible for most so-called ordinary Christians to get on with their lives without being too bothered about such things, but only if they are prepared to bury their heads in the sand. Besides, many ordinary Christians are frequently closer to these matters than we give them credit for. Indeed, a constant criticism I hear from informed lay people is that their spiritual leaders fail to address the kind of challenges that they are already encountering in the world of work. They often feel unsupported in coping with everyday matters that place them very firmly on the exposed, but not always recognised, frontline of mission.

What, for instance, has the gospel of God to say to parents who have to give or withhold permission for the machine, supporting the life of their young daughter, to be switched off? And what has it to say to the medical team who have to pull the plug? How is the Christian message to guide, support and restore the person who is commissioned by his business organisation to make twenty thousand employees redundant? What are the boundaries beyond which the childless couple may not go in their attempt to produce a baby they can call their own? Where is the acceptable dividing line between a full-blown policy of euthanasia and enabling terminally ill people to die with dignity? Has the Bible said the last word on sexuality or may moral theologians and psychologists yet discover that certain aspects of sexuality are as innate for many homosexual people as they are for heterosexual people?

It may be true that few reading this book will be intimately involved in some of the issues mentioned above. However, given the current speed of change, which is likely to increase rather than decrease in the years ahead, most of us will know or be in touch with someone who is deeply involved in such matters. Of one thing we can be sure. Since, as we believe, Jesus is Lord, none of these things is outside his interest and concern. Some will see his, and the Bible's, teaching on such issues as clear and unequivocal. Others will not. Many will struggle to relate scripture, tradition and reasoned reflection on experience, in trying to discern the mind of Christ.

The Church needs to be grateful that God in every age has called and equipped certain people to grapple with such issues, to explore beyond the safety and security of present boundaries and, amidst the complexities of a rapidly changing world, to pioneer the way towards a fresh understanding and expression of Christian truth. Such people often risk their reputation and frequently have to endure criticism, ridicule and abuse. They are seen as betrayers of faith and disturbers of the faithful. They need our support, our understanding and prayers, just as much as we need their moral courage.

Not all boundaries, of course, are to be ignored. Most are there for our guidance, protection and help. They save us from much confusion and chaos. Many of them are vital to our personal survival. They indicate where our responsibility begins and, mercifully, where it ends. Though I am not a Londoner, in the words of the famous cockney song, 'I love London Town' – all of it. Nevertheless, every time I cross from the southern to the northern bank of the River Thames I am aware of a kind of psychological release. The Thames marks the northern boundary of the Diocese of Southwark and, therefore, the limits of my official ecclesiastical responsibility. As I arrive on the 'North Bank' I am pleased to say a prayer for my episcopal brother of London, but I am delighted to recall that he is in charge and not me! Boundaries of this kind help to keep one sane. They declare that there really is a limit to one's responsibilities.

## A proud pedigree

However, there are boundaries which need to be confronted because they have become barriers to the advancement of the Kingdom of God. The practice of breaking through such boundaries for the sake of others, and for the sake of truth and justice, has a proud and distinguished pedigree. It stretches from Moses and the Exodus, through Paul's confrontation with fellow Christians over circumcision and William Wilberforce's attack on the slave trave, to Archbishop Desmond Tutu's moral courage in challenging the evil of apartheid. But it is not only at this macro level that such things happen. They need to happen and do happen at the micro level in the lives of ordinary people in the

Church and in the nation. Many of the things we now take for granted, like the ministry of women, for instance, have come about only through pain and struggle. But the process began when someone had the moral courage to step across the boundary and challenge custom and convention.

I recall a painful period some twenty-five years ago when I had a male assistant curate and two deaconesses as part of my staff team in a Midlands parish. When it came to attending a quarterly Deanery Chapter meeting convened for all ordained clergy, custom allowed me to bring my male colleague with me but refused permission for me to bring my two female colleagues. Clearly the powers that be had tradition on their side in maintaining such an exclusive attitude and when I challenged it I was made to feel somewhat of a trouble-maker. It simply wasn't cricket to flout custom and convention in this way. In response I did the hitherto unthinkable and refused to attend meetings unless all the members of my team were permitted to accompany me. I felt awful about being awkward, but my boundary breaking, or stubbornness, had the desired effect. I don't know if I did my staff team any favours for some deanery meetings can be a great test of patience, but I believed that there was a point of principle at stake as well as an issue of truth and justice. At a distance of twenty-five years that little scenario may not appear significant but at the time it was a fairly major breakthrough.

We can settle for a quiet life and learn to accept customs and conventions which, however traditional and hitherto acceptable, only serve to hinder the cause of Christ and the progress of the Kingdom. But, if we are going to follow Jesus in his suffering love today, we need to remind ourselves that he was prepared to be a disturber of the *status quo* and to step across boundaries of tradition and propriety in order to bring light and salvation to those who felt their need of it. Following such an example we shall discover, more than likely, that God is there before us and, once again, we are simply catching up with him.

## Breaking new ground

That God is often there before us is a truth not only borne out by experience but also, it seems, by sober statistics. Grace Davie's recent sociological study *Religion in Britain since 1945* is a case in point.[4] Subtitled 'Believing without Belonging', Davie's book demonstrates that while church membership and religious practice have both markedly declined in this country since the Second World War, the sense of the sacred is strangely persistent. There are many people in their own, sometimes confused, ways who believe – or who want to believe – without belonging to the institutional Church. Contrary to what experience seems to suggest, over seventy per cent of people in this country are said to profess a belief in God, though only ten per cent of these are church-goers.

These facts resonate with what I find as I move across a fairly wide spectrum of society. Lying not too far beneath the surface of so much unease is a renewed search for meaning. There is a spiritual quest, often expressed in unusual ways – like New Age, alternative therapies and the like – which in reality is a homesickness for God. Underneath the decline in church attendance there is also a marked growth in the religious quest. I find evidence of this in the Church, on the fringes of the Church and far removed from the Church. Such things present the Church with both a challenge and an opportunity. We need to help those who are searching to give a name to the sense of the sacred in their lives to discover and name that name.

Sadly, one of Grace Davie's findings is that within the

Church there has been a loss of belief in the reality of God. Too often there is a 'worthy humanism with a vaguely religious veneer' which passes for worship.[5] Symptomatic signs of this are prayers directed more towards the congregation than they are towards God and implicit suggestions in prayers and sermons that 'God' is no more than an aspect of ourselves. So often such things are done to be relevant. But if Davie's findings are correct, these things are not relevant for they do not fit the religious instincts and needs of the 'believing but not belonging' majority. Surely, in the light of her findings, the greatest need is not for relevance but for pertinence. A more fitting and effectual response to her findings would be a recovery of nerve in the reality of God; a recovery of confident belief in the real God who has made himself known in the life and death and Resurrection of Jesus, and whose Spirit is our living resource. This would be a proper and pertinent response to the persistence of faith in our modern society.

## Alternative ways of being the Church

If we are to take seriously the questions being posed to the Church by the many who believe but do not belong, we must search urgently and creatively for appropriate solutions and be prepared to break new ground in order to find them. In doing so we will have to come to terms with two facts of modern life. First, we live in a society where individual choice has been exalted almost to the level of the sacred. Secondly, the institutional Church is no longer a viable option for many in our society who want to believe or who, in a measure, do believe.

The combination of these two facts results in many people picking and choosing where and how, and if, they will find nourishment for the growth of the sacred in their lives. For whatever reason, they do not consider themselves ready for, nor are they attracted by, the panoply of belief and practice in organised religion. They are still a long way off from the level of commitment that is assumed in so much of the Church's liturgy. They perceive, mostly from a distance, how the Church seems to take complete control over the lives of others and are determined not to be imprisoned by the system.

We may find this puzzling. We may find it hurtful. We may find the acceptance of it difficult in terms of our understanding of the biblical doctrine of the Body of Christ. There may be times when we find it downright annoying. But we must not ignore the facts; we must grapple with them and we must encourage, and not condemn, those who are trying creatively to find a way forward, without selling the past.

There are a variety of responses to the challenge. Some will see the Decade of Evangelism as providing a major part of the answer. Unashamed, forthright and intelligent evangelism, they believe, will help turn the tide so that all 'believers will become belongers'. If only! I am an enthusiast for evangelism, but I am also a realist and I believe that such a singular approach would address only part of the challenge.

Another approach is that of church planting, when a significant section of the regular worshipping congregation of the local church moves out permanently in order to help establish a new congregation in another part of the parish or district. The geographical move away from the traditional church building and much of its formal liturgy seems to make a difference to some who hitherto had 'kept their distance'. There have been notable successes in this approach but, despite such encouragements, the majority of the 'believing but not belonging' fringe remain outside the institutional Church, including those newly planted parts of it.

Most local churches will have a strategy to try to ensure that believers become belongers, though they will have varying degrees of success and failure. As a parish minister in seven different churches, most of them in the inner city, I probably saw more people make the journey from the fringe to the centre of the church family by placing a paint brush rather than a prayer book in their hands. Enlisting their help in a practical project often resulted in their dormant faith becoming alive. Asking for their assistance in a non-patronising way, rather like Jesus did at the well of Samaria, was not a threat. Instead it proved to be, as it did for the woman of Samaria, the beginning of a journey that enlightened and enlarged the faith that was already there. Once again it was a matter of catching up with God.

## Tolerance and acceptance

However, as Grace Davie suggests, we must be cautious about too rigid a use of the terms 'believing' and 'belonging'. It would be a mistake to get over-anxious about them and to make too sharp a distinction between the two categories. Of course, we are not required to suspend our critical faculties or our powers of discernment, but it is usually wiser to leave definitive judgement on such things to God.

In my dreams I have always held the ideal of batwing doors as being the most suitable for our churches. They have so many advantages and they communicate beyond language. They make it easy to get in and out. They don't imprison. The fact that they swing in both directions indicates the balance that is to be kept between worship on the one hand and service to the community on the other. They speak of freedom to belong or not to belong and, unlike most other doors, they do not form a rigid line between those who are 'in' and those who are 'out'.

Jesus had some interesting things to say in this connection to his disciples James and John when they began living up to their name Boanerges, or 'Sons of Thunder'. Having been sent on a mission by Jesus they were annoyed that those to whom they had been sent failed to get the message and refused to respond in the expected and appropriate manner. James and John found it difficult to accept this implied insult to Jesus and the apparent failure of their mission. They reacted in a spirit of intolerance and earned a sharp rebuke from Jesus for their suggestion that revenge should be taken on the villagers concerned.[6] John made a similar mistake when he discovered a man, who was not a known disciple, casting out demons in the name of Jesus. His reaction was predictable, 'We told him to stop because he was not one of us'. Our Lord's response was enlightening: 'Do not stop him . . . whoever is not against us is for us.'[7]

These things suggest to me that what is required is a spirit of tolerance and acceptance towards those who believe but don't, according to our criteria, belong. I believe that the onus is on the Church to find new and imaginative ways to be the Church so that such people may feel included rather than excluded. This will involve the Church not only in breaking new ground but also, perhaps, in repenting of some old attitudes.

One such attitude consists of assuming that people who don't belong, don't believe and therefore the only approach to them must be to seek their conversion. How much better to respond to the challenge and opportunity they represent in terms of the one who said, 'I believe, help me where my faith falls short' (Mark 9:24). Such an attitude places us alongside them rather than over against them, for we also need to grow in faith. Such an attitude makes it possible for the Church to lay aside its institutional 'face', and its implied appeal to 'come and join us', and move out into the community to stand and work alongside those whose faith is real but needs strengthening, whose belief is genuine but needs focusing. All around us there are people, just like us, trying to make sense of their lives in the midst of a complex society, struggling to make their marriages work and their finances stretch. There are people wrestling with the problem of wayward children or broken homes and there are those who stand by helplessly while their loved ones die of a terminal illness. There are thousands trying to cope with unemployment and the demoralisation that goes with it, and there are others who, against all the odds and the power of impersonal forces, are trying to maintain proper standards and values in the work that they do.

It is alongside such people, people like us, that the Church needs to be – and in a form that is accepting and accessible. New venues and times will have to be found, other than Sundays at ten o'clock in the parish church, to make such encounter possible. New methods of listening and communication will have to be tried. Opportunities will have to be provided for people to grapple with issues that concern them – issues, for instance, that are being raised by modern films, medical science or the consumer society. And all needs to be within an affirming atmosphere where doubts can be expressed freely and where Kingdom standards and values can be expressed in a non-aggressive manner.

Some local churches have already caught the vision of this way of being the Church and are devising programmes and strategies to stimulate and strengthen the persistent belief of those who don't belong. Such a policy is not centred on the parish church but rather in cinemas, community halls, civic centres and, frequently, in ordinary homes. It can take the form of lectures, discussions, debates, entertainment or family gatherings. It is not designed to be an evangelistic mission from 'us' to 'them'. Rather, it is the Servant Church making itself available to offer service towards the health and wholeness of communities and individuals.

One such experiment, currently under way in one South London parish, is called 'The Picture Palace'. It provides a chance for people who believe in God, but for one reason or another have not found themselves at ease in attending church regularly, to do something positive about their faith. This has more to do with exploring latent spirituality together than proselytizing. It simply invites people to explore what society has positively discouraged them from exploring in recent years. It tries to present a completely alternative style of worship – 'no hymns . . . no collection . . . no bull' – for people who find the culture of conventional church services so divorced from the culture they are used to that they cannot relate the one to the other. It recognises that the concept of committing oneself to coming week by week to any event is alien to the culture of many people and, therefore, it is flexible and sensitive in its programming. Professional publicity, an attractive and non-threatening place to meet, informal drop-in facilities and community activities during weekdays, an imaginative and comprehensive programme of events – and an overall lightness of touch – are the key elements.

Experiments like this are beginning to emerge across the country. Some are relatively flourishing, some are struggling and some have folded, but the risks are well worth taking, not only for the sake of those who believe 'out there' in the wider community but also for those who 'belong' within the local church.

There is need, however, in all imaginative ventures of

this kind, for creative support, careful monitoring and appropriate accountability. The dismay and distress caused by some aspects of the much publicised Nine O'Clock Service contains some salutary lessons which must not be ignored. At the same time we must not allow the exceptional and unacceptable features of that particular experience to deflect us from exploring how we can best encourage and enable those who believe in, and wish to worship, God, but who, for whatever reason, are not yet ready for traditional Church structures or patterns of worship.

## Grassroots church communities

Another way of being the Church is that of the grassroots church communities, sometimes known as Base Communities. Such communities flourish in Latin America and it is from that part of the world that the title 'A new way of being the Church' has emerged. Their experience may have something to offer us in Britain and in this country such communities are slowly beginning to develop in both urban and rural parishes. Through these groups Christians are discovering ways of sharing their lives, to read the Bible from the perspective of their own situation and to pray and worship together. They are also discovering new ways of engagement with the local community from which the institutional Church had largely been alienated.

The purpose of such groups is to discover empowerment, enabling them to work together in building community and seeking to transform situations of injustice in the neighbourhoods where people live. Here is a description of one such community that met on a South London housing estate:

The struggle against apathy, theft, vandalism and violence as well as the grinding pressures of the hostile
enviroment, unemployment and the more immediate
concerns of family welfare, health and safety, always gave
the fortnightly meetings a certain fragility. Good things
happened. People grew to trust each other, significantly
on one occasion with the key to a neighbour's house in
a neighbourhood where neighbours were most likely to
be burglars! Personal story telling, prayer, reflecting on
the bible and action in the community gradually began
to go hand in hand.[8]

This is just one imaginative attempt at being the Church
in a new way. Of course there are risks involved, as in the
Picture Palace model above, and such groups may in
the short term meet with more apparent failure than success. But it is worth persevering and it is encouraging to
know that the 'grassroots' concept is being taken seriously
within some parts of the institutional Church. 'Such
grassroots church communities are not Church movements
as such, nor neatly defined pastoral models. They are an
attempt to reinterpret the religion of people.'[9] As such they
may provide a serious response to the challenge and opportunity presented by those who believe without belonging.
Whether that response will succeed or not, it represents a
serious attempt at finding a new way to be the Church and
has all the marks of following Jesus in his suffering love.
Certainly it makes the Church less in control and more
vulnerable but, by the same token, more accessible.

## A church evangelised

Perhaps that leads us to consider an even more fundamental matter regarding new ways to be the Church. The tendency is to assume that people have moved away from the Church but what if the real problem has been that the Church has moved away from people: moved away in the sense that it has become less accessible to them; moved away in the sense that it has become preoccupied with saving its own life? If that is the case then 'it is time for the church to be evangelised by the world'.[10] In other words the Church must rediscover the life of Christ, as we discern his hand in our created and world history.

All of us know that the Church is not yet what it is called to be. Frankly, we are sometimes downright ashamed that it is not even what it frequently claims to be. We take comfort in the fact that, by the grace of God and the power of his Spirit, one day it will become what God intends it to be. But the more immediate and pressing question is, 'What should the Church be like in order to pursue God's mission as we move towards the third millennium of Christianity?'

When those early disciples were confronted by the risen Jesus they didn't immediately recognise him. He was the same Jesus only different. He was the transformed Jesus. That was also true of the disciples in the aftermath of the Resurrection and Pentecost. They were transformed – the same people, but radically different. Today's Church needs to enter afresh into that same experience of transformation by the power of God's Spirit – the same Church of our fathers, but radically different in order to meet the challenges for such a time as this. Some words of Vincent Donovan, indicating the kind of Church he would like to see as we approach the end of the twentieth century and the beginning of the third millennium, may yet prove prophetic: 'It will be a church come of age, under the control of the unpredictable Spirit. It will be a risen church born anew out of the death of the one we now know. The pilgrimage along the road to that church will not be a serene and painless journey. Before we reach the end of that road to a church refounded for our age, there will lie a cross, a crucifixion, not for others but for us.'[11] That is the way of suffering love.

### From every kind of fear

Jesus pursued the way of suffering love for the salvation of all people and, indeed, of all things. This is the ultimate goal of mission for both God and his Church. But what does salvation mean in the context of today's world? A scholarly and comprehensive answer to that question has been given in a recent book produced by the Doctrine Commission of the Church of England. It is a superb treatment of the subject, worthy of detailed study and attention. It will prove to be a source for the Church in the years ahead.

For the purpose of this book, however, I want to suggest that salvation means deliverance from every kind of fear. The purists might wish to quibble with such a definition but I believe it would be accepted by many in the Church and understood by many outside it. It also has a foundation in scripture.

I am fascinated by the repeated use by Jesus of the terms 'do not be afraid' and 'go in peace' in the gospels.[12] I know, of course, that there were specific contextual reasons for this but I am still left with the strong conviction that the work that Jesus had come to accomplish through his birth, death and Resurrection had much to do with deliverance from fear and the imparting of peace. The abolition of fear and its replacement by peace seems to me to be a key element in the mission of Jesus – a fact, I believe, borne out by much New Testament teaching and some clear Old Testament indications.

One of the most dramatic and colourful passages of the whole Bible is Psalm 107 – and it is about salvation! Each of its four magnificent word pictures – of exhausted travellers lost in the desert, of prisoners chained in a dungeon, of the sick overshadowed by death and of the sailors fearing for their life in a storm at sea – has a happy ending! All four threatened tragedies end with this formula and these words: 'Then they cried out to the Lord in their trouble, and he delivered them from their distress.' In their fear, the lost travellers, the prisoners, the diseased and the panic-stricken sailors, cried to God for help and he brought them salvation, he delivered them from fear of disaster.

Of course, we must resist the temptation to identify God only with those situations we can't handle ourselves. A God of the gaps theology is foreign to scripture. The gospel has a message for people in their strength as well as in their weakness. But the scriptures reveal God as one who can deliver people not only from their sin but also from their felt need. Salvation for the travellers who were lost meant being directed to the city. Salvation for the prisoners meant being set free. Salvation for the sick meant being made well. Salvation for the storm-tossed sailors meant being rescued from the sea. Salvation is not just for the soul, but for the whole of us in every situation.

The same truth is found in the New Testament. In the epistles, and particularly in the writings of St Paul, salvation is used in a strictly religious sense, though there are exceptions.[13] Salvation is through faith in Christ and is largely restricted to religious experience. It is spoken of as deliverance from sin and so it is, for in Christ God does deliver us from the power of sin. At his birth the message was clear and unequivocal, 'He shall save his people from their sin'. But, if we are true to scripture, salvation is also deliverance from our felt need in those situations where we need to cry to God for help. In the synoptic gospels, for instance, the word for saved (*sozo*) is used in a very wide sense to include deliverance of various kinds, including deliverance from illness, blindness, storms and demons.[14]

There is a comprehensiveness about salvation that is concerned for the total person and for the wholeness of creation. That is why the scope of the Church's mission must be universal in character. 'Salvation is as coherent, broad, and deep as the needs and exigencies of human existence. Mission, therefore, means being involved in the ongoing dialogue between God, who offers his salvation, and the world, which enmeshed in all kinds of evil, craves that salvation.'[15] Mission means being sent to proclaim in deed and word that Christ died and rose again for the life of the world, that he lives to transform human lives and to overcome death. There is no greater privilege than being involved with God and his Church in that all-embracing task.

As Christians we hold the 'One day' vision. One day, God will wipe away all tears; one day, God will abolish all disease; one day, God will overcome all evil in individuals and in society; one day, we shall be delivered from fear of every kind – epitomised by swords being beaten into ploughshares, wolves living peacefully with lambs, young cows, lions and children playing happily together, men and women living in peace – and no one living in fear![16]

But, in the meantime, mission demands that we do all in our power to realise that vision now. To get involved in mission is to get involved in the ministry of salvation. And, for this, there is no time like the present. Indeed, for us, there is no time but the present. We are called for such a time as this.

## Study session

OPENING PRAYER

> Vulnerable God,
> You took the risk of flesh for our salvation.
> Help us to take the risk of faith
> For the salvation of your world.

READINGS

John 20:19–23; Mark 9:38–40.

MEDITATIONS

'Following Jesus in his suffering love was a risky business in the Early Church. It still is today.' (p. 166)

'The scars of crucifixion and death that [Christ] revealed in his hands and side were not only proofs of his identity, they indicated a cost to be expected by those whom he commissions.' (p. 167)

'When God became human he also became vulnerable.' (p. 167)

'Jesus not only comes to his Church in word and sacrament . . . he also comes in unlikely people and places.' (p. 169)

'Love constrained Jesus to set aside convention and custom if these things got in the way of grace and mercy, forgiveness and justice.' (p. 171)

'The onus is on the Church to find new and imaginative ways of being the Church.' (p. 181)

OUR EXPERIENCE (IN PAIRS)

• Where are the unlikely people and places through whom God may be calling our church community?

• How are lay Christians best supported in the challenges to faith which face them through the world of work?

• What are we saved from and to do? (pp. 187ff.) What difference does this make for us and the mission of the Church?

CHRISTIAN RESPONSE (AS A GROUP)

• 'The Church is not yet what it is called to be. It is not even what it frequently claims to be. But by the grace of God and the power of his Spirit, one day it will become what God intends it to be.' (p. 186) What is the 'one day' vision in your church? (p. 189)

• What will equip us best to respond to that 'homesickness for God' we find around us? (pp. 177ff.)

• What changes in structure or style will be required for the Church facing the new millennium? Where will our pictures, clues and inspiration come from? (p. 178ff.)

ACTION

• Devise a strategy for helping believers to become belongers. (p. 180)

• Meet and pray with other local churches to explore mission 'beyond the boundaries'.

CLOSING PRAYER

God of all,
When we were still far off
You came and met us in your Son.
Send us out
To meet and welcome
Those longing for your love.
In the name of Christ. Amen.

'Mission is the church crossing frontiers in the form of a servant.' (David Bosch)

# References

## Introduction

1. I am grateful to Simon Barrow, Adult Education and Training Officer in the Diocese of Southwark, for his help in connection with the Study session material.
2. This prayer, based on the Bishop of Southwark's Mission Statement, was written by Canon David Atkinson, Chancellor of Southwark Cathedral and Canon Missioner.

## Chapter 1

1. David Bosch, *Transforming Mission* (Orbis Books, 1992), p. 10
2. Senior and Stuhlmueller, *The Biblical Foundations for Mission* (SCM, 1983), p. 3
3. John Goldingay, *God's Prophet, God's Servant* (Paternoster Press, 1994), p. 95
4. Isaiah 42:1–8
5. Senior and Stuhlmueller, op. cit., p. 154
6. See Mark 7:24–30 and Matthew 8:5–13
7. See Matthew 22 and Luke 14
8. Luke 15
9. Matthew 28:16–20
10. 2 Corinthians 5:14
11. Emil Brunner, *The Word and the World* (SCM, 1931), p. 108
12. Esther 4:14

13. *The New International Dictionary of the New Testament*, Vol. 3 (Paternoster Press, 1978), p. 837
14. Professor J. Jeremias commenting on Mark 1:15 in *New Testament Theology* (SCM, 1971)
15. Bosch, op. cit., p. 2
16. Dietrich Bonhoeffer, *Letters from prison* (SCM, 1971)
17. Bosch, op. cit., p. 512
18. Ibid., p. 518
19. Senior and Stuhlmueller, op. cit., p. 340
20. Ibid., p. 341
21. For the whole passage see John 12:20–33

## Chapter 2

1. Eucharistic Prayer of Thanksgiving, The Alternative Service Book 1980
2. Luke 9:28–43
3. St John of the Cross
4. Bosch, op. cit., p. 472
5. Bonhoeffer, quoted by Robrect Michiels, *The Self-Understanding of the Church after Vatican Two*, Louvain Studies, Vol. 14 (1989)
6. Philippians 3:12, NEB Revised (free translation)
7. General Confession, The Book of Common Prayer
8. Report of the Archbishop of Canterbury's Commission on Urban Priority Areas, 1985
9. 'And can it be', Charles Wesley, Hymns & Psalms 216
10. 1 Peter 2:9
11. Bosch, op. cit., p. 472
12. Andrew F. Walls, *British Missions*, Vol. 6 (International Bulletin of Missionary Research, 1982)
13. 1 Corinthians 12; Romans 12; Ephesians 4; 1 Peter 4
14. Quoted by J. W. de Gruchy, *Theology and Ministry in Context and Crisis* (Collins, 1987)
15. Lesslie Newbigin, *Mission in Christ's Way* (WCC, 1987)
16. *All Are Called*, Report to General Synod, 1985
17. Cf. Richard J. Mouw, *Called to Holy Worldliness*, Laity Exchange Books (Fortress Press, 1980)

18. Ibid.
19. Bosch, op. cit., p. 472
20. Luke 11:1
21. John V. Taylor, *The Go Between God* (SCM, 1972), p. 1

**Chapter 3**

1. John V. Taylor, *Kingdom Come* (SCM, 1989)
2. John Stott, *Christian Counter Culture* (Inter-Varsity Press, 1978), p. 172
3. Luke 24:19; Matthew 18:23–25; Luke 10:25–37
4. Isaiah 33:17 and 22; cf. 32:1
5. Luke 15
6. Matthew 20:1–15
7. E.g. Mark 2:23–28, 3:1–6; Matthew 23:23, 22:40
8. Leonardo Boff, *Jesus Christ, Liberator* (SPCK, 1980), p. 55
9. Hans Kung, *On Being a Christian* (Collins, 1977), p. 231
10. Stott, op. cit.
11. Matthew 22:1–14
12. John 13; cf. Mark 10:42–45
13. Lesslie Newbigin, *The Open Secret* (SPCK, 1978)
14. Eric James, *A Life of John Robinson* (Collins, 1987), p. 50
15. *The Truth Shall Make You Free: The Lambeth Conference 1988* (Anglican Consultative Council, 1988), para. 70
16. Russell Barry, *The Relevance of the Church* (Nisbet & Co., 1935), p. 190
17. *The Truth Shall Make You Free*, para. 8
18. Walter Brueggemann, *Prophetic Imagination* (Fortress Press, 1978), pp. 11ff.

**Chapter 4**

1. Matthew 5:15, J. B. Phillips, *New Testament in Modern English* (Collins, 1960)
2. John 8:28, 14:9; cf. v. 24
3. 1 Peter 2:4; Ephesians 5:15; 2 Peter 3:18
4. Ephesians 4:14ff.
5. Jude 3 (New Jerusalem Bible)

6. David Bleakley in CMS Newsletter No. 522

7. *The Hodder Book of Christian Quotations* (Hodder, 1983)

8. John 8:12

9. Matthew 5:14

10. *The Truth Shall Make You Free*, Resolution 43

11. William J. Abraham, *The Logic of Evangelism* (Hodder, 1989)

12. Professor Walter Hollenweger, *Evangelism Today* (Christian Journals, Belfast, 1976)

13. Ephesians 4:22–23 and 25ff.; 5:2, 8, 15; 5:21–6:9; 6:10ff. and 3:10

14. Mark 10:46–end

15. Pope Paul VI

16. The Revd Graham Cray, Public Lecture

17. 2 Corinthians 4:7

18. Mark 5:21–34

19. 1 Thessalonians 1:4–10

20. *My Fair Lady*, the musical adaptation of George Bernard Shaw's *Pygmalion*

21. Kahlil Gibran, *The Prophet* (Heinemann, 1926)

22. Acts 2:12

23. Archbishop Robert Runcie, Address to General Synod

24. Ephesians 2:10 (Revised English Bible and Jerusalem Bible)

## Chapter 5

1. John 16:13

2. John 8:32

3. John 18:32–38

4. Luke 15:11–24

5. John 14:6

6. 1 John 1:1–4 (John Stott, *Tyndale Commentary*, Tyndale Press, 1964)

7. L. Griffiths, *The Eternal Legacy* (Hodder & Stoughton, 1963), p. 102

8. Luke 24:13–35

9. 2 Timothy 1:14

10. 2 Timothy 2:15; 4:2ff.

11. A. McGrath, *Bridge-Building: Effective Christian Apologetics* (Inter-Varsity Press, 1992), p. 206

12. Ramsey, Address to British Association, 1959

13. Hans Kung, *Global Responsibility* (SCM, 1992), p. xv

14. Michael Ramsey, *Canterbury Essays and Addresses* (SPCK, 1964)

15. Michael Ramsey, *Introducing the Christian Faith* (SCM, XPRESS reprint 1994)

16. Colossians 1:15–20

17. John 14:9–10

18. Bosch, op. cit., p. 513

19. John 20:19, 20

20. 1 Corinthians 15:12–19

21. Frances Young and David Ford, *Meaning and Truth in 2 Corinthians* (SPCK, 1987)

22. Romans 12:8 (NIV); cf. Acts 4:12

23. Acts 9:10–19

24. Acts 11:19–end

## Chapter 6

1. Luke 10:27–37

2. Luke 22:27

3. Luke 8:42b–48; John 9:1–12

4. T. W. Manson, *The Teaching of Jesus* (Cambridge University Press, 1931)

5. John 13:1–17

6. Mark 10:45

7. Micah 6:8

8. Stephen Winward, *A Guide to the Prophets* (Hodder & Stoughton, 1968), p. 69

9. Matthew 22:34–40; Mark 12:28–34

10. Ephesians 4:15, 1:10; cf. Colossians 1:20

11. Mark 10:46–52

12. Michael Paget Wilkes, *Poverty, Revolution and the Church* (Paternoster Press, 1981), p. 75

13. Henri Nouwen, *With Burning Hearts* (Geoffrey Chapman, 1994), p. 89

14. Bosch, op. cit., p. 435
15. Deuteronomy 24; Psalm 72:12–14; Micah 6:8
16. Luke 4:16–21
17. Leviticus 25:8–end
18. Peter Cotterell, *Mission and Meaninglessness* (SPCK, 1990), p. 194
19. Cf. Bosch, op. cit., p. 412
20. Ibid., p. 437
21. Ephesians 6:10–18
22. Luke 1:46–55
23. Mark 10:17–22
24. Alex Vidler, *Church in an Age of Revolution* (Penguin, 1990)
25. Bosch, op. cit., p. 437
26. Galatians 5:6

## Chapter 7

1. Cf. John 20:19–23
2. Matthew 25:31–end
3. John 4:4–30
4. Grace Davie, *Religion in Britain since 1945* (Blackwell, 1994)
5. Ibid., p. 93
6. Mark 3:17; Luke 9:34
7. Mark 9:38–40; Luke 9:49–50
8. Canon Peter Price, General Secretary, USPG, in *Scargill Newsletter*, September 1995
9. Canon Peter Price, in *Christian Issues*, 1 (1991)
10. Vincent J. Donovan, *The Church in the Midst of Creation* (SCM, 1989)
11. Ibid.
12. Matthew 14:22–33; Mark 5:32–34; Luke 7:50; John 20:19, 21, 26
13. Cf. Acts 27:34; Philippians 1:18; 1 Timothy 2:15; 2 Timothy 4:18; Hebrews 11:7; James 5:15
14. Luke 7:15; Mark 10:52; Matthew 14:22–33; cf. Mark 6:45–51, 5:1–20
15. Bosch, op. cit., p. 400
16. Micah 4:1–5; Isaiah 2:2–4, 11:6–9